Teaching Plagiarism Prevention to College Students

Teaching Plagiarism Prevention to College Students

An Ethics-Based Approach

Connie Strittmatter
Virginia K. Bratton

ROWMAN & LITTLEFIELD
Lanham • Boulder • New York • London

Published by Rowman & Littlefield
A wholly owned subsidary of The Rowman & Littlefield Publishing Group, Inc.
4501 Forbes Boulevard, Suite 200, Lanham, Maryland 20706
www.rowman.com

Unit A, Whitacre Mews, 26-34 Stannary Street, London SE11 4AB

British Library Cataloguing in Publication Information Available

Library of Congress Cataloging-in-Publication Data

Names: Strittmatter, Connie, author. | Bratton, Virginia K., 1973- author.
Title: Teaching plagiarism prevention to college students : an ethics-based
   approach / Connie Strittmatter and Virginia K. Bratton.
Description: Lanham, Maryland : Rowman & Littlefield, 2016. | Includes
   bibliographical references and index.
Identifiers: LCCN 2016012049 (print) | LCCN 2016024226 (ebook) | ISBN
   9781442264403 (cloth : alk. paper) | ISBN 9781442264410 (pbk. : alk.
   paper) | ISBN 9781442264427 (electronic)
Subjects: LCSH: Plagiarism—Prevention. | Plagiarism—Moral and ethical
   aspects. | Education, Higher—Moral and ethical aspects. | Student ethics.
Classification: LCC PN167 .S77 2016 (print) | LCC PN167 (ebook) | DDC
   808.02/50711—dc23
LC record available at https://lccn.loc.gov/2016012049

Printed in the United States of America

This book is dedicated to intentional plagiarists, both students and professionals, who are too numerous to name here. May this book help instructors to decrease your numbers in the future.

Contents

Figures

Tables and Textboxes

TABLES

TEXT BOXES

Preface

Apologize for what? I'd do it again!

—Self-reported cheater[1]

When you get to college, you don't follow the same rules your parents laid down for you. But we're just taking a break. We'll likely get back to the rules later.

—Accounting student at the University of Dayton[2]

The quotes above demonstrate the mind-set of some college students when it comes to how they perceive cheating. While these comments may not necessarily represent the majority voice of today's college students, increasing rates of academic misconduct[3] cause us to conclude that these attitudes pervade the typical college campus. Academic misconduct is at the forefront of issues being addressed by university administrators and faculty. This book addresses a specific type of academic misconduct, plagiarism, and extends the existing body of literature that provides innovative ways to deliver plagiarism prevention instruction.

The goal of this book is to introduce a new approach for delivering plagiarism prevention instruction. The majority of plagiarism prevention instruction focuses on aiding the *unintentional plagiarist*. These students do not understand how to cite sources properly, paraphrase, and properly attribute sources in a research paper. This type of instruction is very important to helping ensure that students are equipped to handle rigorous assignments during their academic careers. However, as suggested by the quotes above, there is an academic underworld consisting of students who know how to cite, paraphrase, and attribute sources but do not take the time or care to do so. We refer to these students as *intentional plagiarists*. They may know that plagiarism is viewed unfavorably by their university, but as students, they view it differently. For these students, plagiarizing materials and submitting work that is not their own is not morally wrong. With this firmly held stance, it is difficult to persuade them otherwise. It is unlikely that plagiarism prevention instruction that focuses on the mechanics of writing will change their attitudes toward plagiarism.

This book presents an instructional approach that we designed to address these intentional plagiarists. In our experiences in higher education, we frequently observed instructors who tell students that plagiarism is an ethical violation but fail to explain why it is a violation. Combining our interests in business ethics research and library instruction, our approach emerged from a research study that we initiated in 2010 to examine student academic behavior from an ethics perspective. In this research, we developed and applied training intervention on students enrolled in writing-intensive courses. We found that students were less likely to view plagiarism as an ethical issue before the training intervention. However, after they received the training, their ethical perceptions of plagiarism increased. We also collected anecdotal evidence from collaborative instructors indicating that student incidents of plagiarism decreased in their classes after we provided this training.

These experiences motivated us to formalize this training into a program aimed at the intentional student plagiarist. The Plagiarism and Ethics Awareness Training (PEAT) is a curriculum designed to help students critically think about why plagiarism is unethical. In this program, we ask students to analyze plagiarism using a series of ethical criteria as a benchmark. Through a series of experiential activities, this program seeks to guide students to the conclusion that *plagiarism is an unethical behavior*. By changing student attitudes toward this behavior, our hope is that we can effect behavioral change leading to a pronounced decrease in plagiarism rates in academic contexts.

This book is intended primarily for librarians who provide plagiarism prevention instruction to students as well as any instructor in a writing-intensive course who seeks to prevent acts of plagiarism. Many of the principles and strategies described in this book can be used by instructors who wish to integrate a module on plagiarism and the ethics of plagiarism into his or her course. The assessment portion of this book (chapters 6 to 8) can be beneficial to any group administering a program and needing to evaluate and report the results of their program.

This book is organized into three parts. Part I of the book consists of two chapters that serve as introductory and background material that lay the framework for PEAT. Chapter 1 reviews the current state of academic integrity within the academic institution. The chapter begins by providing an overview of the reasons for academic misconduct. From there, we narrow the focus from academic misconduct to plagiarism specifically. We discuss the characteristics of unintentional and intentional plagiarists. We review the literature on existing plagiarism prevention strategies, including teaching strategies, assignment design, conduct codes, and detection strategies. The chapter concludes with the introduction of the PEAT approach to plagiarism prevention instruction.

We consider chapter 2 a primer on ethical theory. PEAT is grounded in business ethics theory and research. To assist readers who may not have a background in ethics, we felt that a chapter providing some overview of the ethical concepts was prudent. In chapter 2, we discuss the four steps involved in moral development. From there, we summarize the key concepts of the underlying theories used in the modules developed for the curriculum:

- Stakeholder analysis (stakeholder theory)
- Theoretical criteria (multidimensional ethics)
- Practical criteria
- Changing the culture of plagiarism (whistle-blowing theory)
- Giving Voice to Values framework

Part II of the book focuses on the PEAT approach and consists of three chapters. Chapter 3 focuses on the pedagogical strategies for PEAT. The chapter begins with a discussion of the transmissive and transformative approaches to teaching. PEAT uses primarily transformative techniques in the form of case-based discussion and role playing. The chapter focuses on the outcomes of a PEAT session, including acknowledging stakeholders, establishing the university's moral expectations of students, and addressing unethical actions. We then describe the pedagogical relevance of the teaching techniques used to achieve these outcomes successfully. We specifically focus on justifications for the amount of and approach to ethics instruction to provide during an instruction session and the use of discussion and role play in the curriculum.

Chapter 4 describes the PEAT curriculum. We review each module (stakeholder analysis, theoretical criteria, practical criteria, changing the culture of plagiarism, and the Giving Voice to Values framework). In each module, we discuss how you would design and present the module, teaching points you would want to incorporate, and potential pushback you might get from students. In addition, we provide examples of lesson plans based on intracurricular (one-shot library instruction session), intercurricular (multisession module embedded into a course), and extracurricular (e.g., international student orientation) sessions.

In chapter 5, we discuss the finer points of implementing the PEAT program, including how you, as the instructor, can help ensure that the discussions and role-playing activities are successfully facilitated. We also discuss how you might implement PEAT in more challenging teaching sessions, such as online environments and high-enrollment classes (more than 50 students).

In part III, we present an assessment strategy based on Donald Kirkpatrick's four-level evaluation of the training model to evaluate not only the PEAT program but also any training program that you might have. This model begins in chapter 6 with an appraisal of the reactions of training participants and then moves to evaluating what knowledge participants have gained from the PEAT program. Several methods for evaluating the results of plagiarism prevention training are discussed, including how to administer pre- and postsurveys using the Multidimensional Ethics Scale and Theory of Planned Behavior.

In chapter 7, we assume that the PEAT program is provided in conjunction with skills-focused plagiarism prevention instruction, and we discuss how to assess behavioral change among training participants as well as organizational-level results of the training program, including a discussion of how to calculate return on investment.

Finally, in chapter 8, we consider how to communicate the results of the PEAT program to key stakeholders in your organization, which may include college deans, a college's curriculum committee, trainers, and trainees. While the results of your program evaluation do not change, the method for reporting your results will vary on the basis of the stakeholder. This chapter discusses the best strategies for communicating results to stakeholders as well as considerations to guide the communication of both good and bad evaluation results.

A broad range of topics are covered in this book. Topics such as the PEAT curriculum and assessment are covered in depth, as they are the crux of the book. However, the overview of academic integrity and ethics theory is not exhaustive, as their inclusion provides context for the PEAT program. After reading this book, we hope that you will have the tools and strategies needed to implement a PEAT program. We also expect readers to have a more thorough understanding of how to conduct effective and meaningful evaluation of plagiarism prevention training programs.

NOTES

1. Stephen F. Davis, Patrick F. Drinan, and Tricia Bertram Gallant, *Cheating in School: What We Know and What We Can Do* (Malden, MA: Wiley-Blackwell, 2009), 87.

2. L. Berton, "Business Students Hope to Cheat and Prosper a New Study Shows," *Wall Street Journal*, April 25, 1995.

3. Tricia Bertram Gallant, "Twenty-First Century Forces Shaping Academic Integrity," *ASHE Higher Education Report* 33, no. 5 (2008): 65–67, doi:10.1002/aehe.3305.

Acknowledgments

This book would not have been possible without the support of several individuals and groups at Montana State University (MSU). This project evolved from a study that we conducted at MSU from 2009 to 2014. We received funding to conduct this study from several departments at MSU, including the Jake Jabs College of Business and Entrepreneurship, the Renné Library, and the Center for Faculty Excellence. Our research would not have been possible without the collaboration of several business and engineering instructors who allowed us to survey their students and come into their classes to talk about plagiarism: Laura Black, Amber Raile, Joe Eldring, Jeff Heys, Myleen Leary, Hunter Lloyd, Dan Miller, and Terry Profota. We also would like to thank Christine Foreman for involving the College of Engineering in our research and facilitating contacts with instructors in the school.

We extend our appreciation to anonymous reviewers at the *College and Research Libraries* journal for their developmental feedback on our manuscript, which formed the basis for this book.

Finally, we thank our friends and family for their unending support throughout the research and writing process.

I

PLAGIARISM:
AN ETHICAL ISSUE

Plagiarism is one of the more challenging issues facing university administrators and faculty today because there are many reasons why it occurs. In some instances, plagiarism is *unintentional*—the student does not have the skills to appropriately cite and paraphrase resources, and educators can address this problem by providing a plagiarism prevention skills program. Through the course of instruction, we can provide students with information that will enable them to write research papers that are well documented, appropriately attributed, and accurately cited. The more challenging problem for those in higher education is addressing *intentional* plagiarism. Traditional plagiarism prevention instruction will not remedy this problem because intentional plagiarism stems from an attitudinal issue.

Intentional plagiarists often approach college education with a sense of entitlement. Many believe that by merely paying their tuition bill, they are entitled to a college degree. For these students, graduating with a diploma is contingent not on effort but rather on showing up and paying their dues. Intentional plagiarists put in the least amount of work possible because they do not value the process of receiving an education. Therefore, they do not view shortcuts such as plagiarizing assignments as unethical. For these students to modify their behavior, they certainly need a specific set of research and writing skills, but more importantly, their *attitudes* toward learning and plagiarism must change. In part I of this book, we explore *why* an ethical approach to plagiarism prevention is valuable and *how* ethics theories and concepts support this approach.

In chapter 1, after discussing the issues surrounding academic integrity and current plagiarism prevention strategies, we introduce a prevention model to address intentional plagiarism. The Plagiarism and Ethics Awareness Training (PEAT) program focuses on the ethics surrounding plagiarism. In the PEAT approach, students apply ethical principles to a plagiarism scenario to determine if the action presented in the scenario was ethical. If we can convey to students why plagiarism is unethical, then we can shift their perceptions about plagiarism from an acceptable to an unacceptable act.

Because PEAT is rooted in ethical theory, we provide an overview of the origins of ethics and key ethics concepts and theories in chapter 2. These concepts provide the foundation for the PEAT pedagogical and curricular design that is discussed in part II. In chapter 2, we draw on business ethics theory to explain the steps involved in ethical decision making using Rest's model of morality.[1] The four components to this model include (1) moral sensitivity, which is the ability to consider the alternatives to a situation and the impacts it may have on others; (2) moral judgment, or identifying which of the alternative considered is the best option; (3) moral motivation, which prioritizes the moral action over the convenient or selfish action; and (4) moral character, which is the individual's ability to follow through and complete the moral action. We demonstrate how this model of decision making relates to the decisions that students make when contemplating whether to plagiarize a paper or submit their own work.

We then discuss the key concepts used in the development of the PEAT curriculum, including the following:

- Stakeholder theory—evaluating those individuals or groups potentially affected by an action
- Reidenbach and Robin's multidimensional ethics[2]—the utilization of moral equity, cultural relativism, and contractualism for ethical decision making
- Ethical climates within an organization—how an organization's norms toward ethical behavior impact organizational culture
- Practical ethical criteria—tools, such as the front-page-of-the-newspaper test, that can help students make timely ethical decisions
- Whistle-blowing theory—potential obligation that an observer has when responding to and preventing future unethical actions
- Giving voice to values[3]—how to respond to an unethical action

Each of these concepts serves as the basis for the five modules discussed in chapter 4.

NOTES

1. James R. Rest, *Moral Development* (New York: Praeger, 1986).
2. R. Eric Reidenbach and Donald P. Robin, "Toward the Development of a Multidimensional Scale for Improving Evaluations of Business Ethics," *Journal of Business Ethics* 9, no. 8 (1990): 639–53, http://www.jstor.org/stable/25072080.
3. Mary C. Gentile, *Giving Voice to Values: How to Speak Your Mind When You Know What's Right* (New Haven, CT: Yale University Press, 2010).

1

Plagiarism Prevention Instruction

Where Did We Come From?
Where Are We Going?

In chapter 1, we begin with a discussion of academic integrity examining student and situational influences on cheating in an academic context. We then shift our discussion to a subset of academic integrity and the focus of this book: plagiarism. We differentiate intentional plagiarism from unintentional plagiarism and examine traditional approaches to preventing the latter. This chapter highlights a deficiency in plagiarism prevention instruction approaches to address intentional plagiarism and introduces the Plagiarism and Ethics Awareness Training (PEAT) program.

OVERVIEW OF ACADEMIC INTEGRITY IN THE TWENTY-FIRST CENTURY

In an increasingly evolving technical world where crowdsourcing and open-source resources are becoming more prevalent, students are challenged to differentiate between the fine lines of collaboration and collusion. With information easily accessible over the Internet, the understanding of an author's intellectual property is not as clear as it had once been when materials appeared only in a print source.[1] Accompanying a lack of knowledge about what constitutes academic misconduct, there are additional factors that lead to cheating on college campuses. Miller, Murdock, Anderman, and Poindexter have synthesized a plethora of studies exploring cheater characteristics, including gender, race, religion, academic major, intellect, personality type, and motivation, and concluded that the "individual characteristics cannot be completely separated from the context in which the cheating transgression occurs."[2] So, while there may be some traits that may lead to increased cheating behaviors, situational factors may be better predictors of academic misconduct.

Students are under a great deal of pressure to excel academically. Many times, students are struggling to maintain an A average while also participating in community service projects, internships, and university clubs and groups. The juggling of all these activities can lead to time pressures in which something ultimately has to give. The pressures that students feel to be competitive scholastically are not to be dismissed. Competition for scholarships, internships, and admittance into graduate school and securing a well-paying job have increased with the influx of students now going to college.[3] These pressures can result in one of two scenarios. In one scenario, these pressured students are aware of the potential ramifications for cheating behavior. Assuming that they also are conscientious, these students will be less likely to cheat for fear of the potential penalties and how that may affect their goals. In another scenario, pressured students may feel that they lack control over their situations (i.e., they are not able to study because they have to work to pay for tuition), and because of this lack of control, they will resort to cheating out of sheer desperation.[4] Students who are not high academic achievers or are struggling with a course may be more susceptible to cheating. In one study, students indicated that they would be more likely to cheat if they lacked preparation to complete an assignment (14 percent), were likely to fail the class (8 percent), or had difficulty learning the material (8 percent).[5]

Another aspect of situational cheating relates to student motivations in school. If a student's sole interest in attending a university is to secure a diploma rather than to receive an education, then they are more likely to seek opportunities to cheat.[6] However, if students have a general interest in the subject matter and their focus is on learning, then they will be less likely to participate in academic misconduct.[7] Exploring conditions where students are less likely to cheat, one study asked a sample of students, "Are there specific situations in which you would be more or less likely to cheat?" While the majority of the students answered the question by providing situations in which they would be more inclined to cheat, 9 percent of students answered that they would be less likely to cheat if they had an effective teacher (5 percent) or enjoyed the subject matter (4 percent).[8]

Accompanying some of these situational factors is a change in attitudes by students regarding education. In some instances, students view education as a right rather than an earned privilege. By paying tuition, they feel that they should receive a degree regardless of the effort they put forth.[9] This shift in mind-set can often lead to cheating behaviors. The implications that can arise from this are worrisome, as this can have a very real impact on the student, the university, and future employers. If a student expects to receive a degree regardless of his or her effort, then there is likely to be a gap in the knowledge and skill set needed to effectively execute the tasks of a future job. The employer will ultimately feel the ramifications because the student will not be able to perform well in the job he or she was hired for. If the university does not take steps to address the situation and hold students accountable for their academic misbehavior, it risks damaging its reputation.

Regardless of whether academic misconduct occurs due to character traits, situational variables, or a change in attitude by the student population, it is crucial for a university to establish a culture in which academic integrity is at the forefront of its mission.

UNIVERSITY RESPONSE—CONSISTENT ENFORCEMENT OF POLICIES

For students to recognize that plagiarism is an unacceptable practice in an academic setting, there must be a commitment on the part of instructors and university administrators to address academic misconduct violations in a firm and fair manner. In many instances, an instructor may be aware that cheating has occurred but is either not comfortable addressing the behavior or is not equipped to do so. Some reasons cited for not wanting to report an instance of cheating include fear of repercussions for students, lack of concrete evidence, time and effort to report the infraction, and lack of follow-through by administration.[10] Academic misconduct cases vary. Instructors and administrators need to take into account the intent, recurrence, and severity of the act to identify an acceptable penalty,[11] but ultimately a university should commit to establishing an environment that promotes ethical academic behavior. Davis, Drinan, and Gallant offer a four-stage approach to institutionalizing academic integrity in a university setting:[12]

- Stage 1: Recognizing the problem—In this most basic stage, there is recognition among faculty, students, academic support services, and administration that instead of a culture of academic integrity, a culture of academic misconduct prevails. The urgency to address the issue may be triggered by a significant incident (e.g., Harvard's investigation into 125 students involved in cheating and plagiarizing answers on a final exam),[13] but many times it results from a subtle pervasive recognition that the problem exists. In this stage, there is not a cohesive approach to addressing academic misconduct, but there is a desire for the problem to be addressed.[14]
- Stage 2: Identifying solutions to the problem—This stage expands on the first stage because the discussions go beyond watercooler discussions to a more formal discussion within the university setting. During this stage, academic cheating is explored more systematically to identify the extent of the problem. The university (faculty, staff, administrators, and students) recognizes that to effectively address academic cheating, there needs to be a centralized process in place. Academic misconduct policies are created (or resurrected), and a plan is developed conveying the university's commitment to addressing the problem.[15]
- Stage 3: Implementing university-wide policies—Best-laid plans often fall by the wayside when adequate human and monetary resources are not allocated

to them. This step executes the implementation plan. At this point, deans and department chairs must ensure that academic integrity policies are fully integrated into their departments and colleges. The core values of academic integrity are communicated to everyone. Students are educated about how to avoid plagiarism and where the fine lines of collaboration and collusion lie. Systematic training is developed to help faculty understand the policies and how to address instances of cheating. And perhaps most important, this universal commitment establishes a trust relationship between faculty and administrators. Faculty know that they have support from administrators when reporting academic misconduct issues.[16]

- Stage 4: University-wide culture of integrity—This stage is the culmination of the work produced in the first three stages. Academic integrity has been fully integrated into university life in the form of either student-run honor codes or consistently applied university policies. This does not mean that cheating or plagiarizing never happens, but when it does, everyone is aware of the policies in place and feels confident that the case will be addressed in a fair manner.[17]

In the remainder of this chapter, we focus on a subset of academic integrity: plagiarism. Plagiarism is an issue that all universities and colleges must address. Many instructors make attempts to teach students about what plagiarism is, why it is unacceptable, and how to prevent it. Yet plagiarism continues to be a regular occurrence on college campuses. In the paragraphs that follow, we review current strategies to address plagiarism, including strategies such as plagiarism prevention instruction, assignment design, honor codes, and detection strategies. After discussing these strategies, we present a new model of plagiarism instruction that uses an ethical lens when teaching about plagiarism prevention. We begin this discussion by differentiating three categories of plagiarism:

- Unintentional plagiarism
- Intentional plagiarism
- Contextual plagiarism[18]

Unintentional Plagiarism

Unintentional plagiarism occurs when students do not fully understand how to appropriately attribute information that they borrow from others. The plagiarism is not malicious; rather, students lack the knowledge on how to cite sources correctly.[19] Examples of unintentional plagiarism include sham paraphrasing, which occurs when text is copied verbatim and the source is included in the text. Because the verbatim text is not enclosed in quotation marks, writers are misrepresenting the phrasing as their own. Illicit paraphrasing occurs when material is paraphrased but writers do not include an in-text citation to acknowledge that the information was borrowed from another work. Verbatim copying is when writers copy text verbatim and includes no in-text citation, in essence cutting and pasting sections of a paper into their paper.[20] While some may view these as intentional acts of plagiarism, in general these types of plagiarism occur because students do not have a thorough grasp of how to cite sources properly. Students are often confused about what constitutes plagiarism. Although they may be able to identify egregious forms of plagiarism, such as submitting another's paper as their own, some of the nuanced aspects of plagiarism, such as how to paraphrase correctly, may be a mystery to students.[21]

Intentional Plagiarism

Intentional plagiarism is deliberate and malicious. Students intentionally and knowingly copy material from other authors to pass off as their own ideas and writing.[22] Learning is not a motivational factor for students who intentionally plagiarize. Rather, these students plagiarize because they do not recognize the value in accurately representing their writing as their own and attributing sources correctly. They seek to find the quick and easy way to complete an assignment. They also believe that they will not get caught, so to them the risks associated with plagiarizing are worth what they view as the reward.[23] Intentional plagiarism can take on many forms, such as ghostwriting, purloining, consensual sharing, and recycling papers. Ghostwriting is a document written by a third party but submitted as a student's own work. These can either be papers purchased online or taken from a report bank at a place of employment. Students can also take advantage of the work completed by their classmates either with their knowledge or without. Purloining is when students copy an assignment without the other person's knowledge. Consensual sharing of papers is when students copy an assignment with the consent of the other person.[24] Recycling papers occurs when students submit assignments that were originally written for and submitted in one or more different courses. While this is not technically plagiarism, it often violates a university's student academic code of conduct and is in line with the rationale for intentional plagiarism—to not embrace the learning process.

Contextual Plagiarism

Contextual plagiarism occurs because students are not able to effectively manage their time. They intentionally plagiarize, but it is done not maliciously but rather as a result of taking on more than they can handle in both their personal and their academic lives. Students are overwhelmed by the work assigned to them, and as a result they find shortcuts to help them submit assignments by their due date.[25] We may see contextual plagiarism becoming more prevalent with the recent trend in students working full-time while taking classes either part- or full-time.[26] Students will need support to help balance these pressures of juggling multiple tasks.

ADDRESSING PLAGIARISM

Plagiarism prevention efforts should take a multipronged approach to address the various types of plagiarists. First, students need to learn about what constitutes plagiarism and strategies to avoid committing plagiarism. Second, instructors need to have mechanisms in place to help them detect instances of plagiarism. Each of these strategies, as well as several approaches within each strategy, is addressed below.

Plagiarism Prevention Strategies

There are three tactics that instructors can take to prevent the occurrence of plagiarism in their classes. The first two tactics placed the burden of plagiarism prevention on the instructor: teaching plagiarism prevention skills and designing assignments that are harder to plagiarize. The third tactic places the onus on students: integrating a code of ethics into assignment submission.

Teaching Plagiarism Prevention

One aspect of plagiarism prevention is an instructional component. Many students are not familiar with what exactly plagiarism is and, more important, how to not plagiarize. Plagiarism prevention instruction needs to be incorporated into the academic setting, but there are questions about how and where it should be provided. Should it be incorporated into a required writing course? Does each department identify a course in which to provide plagiarism prevention instruction? Does the responsibility lie with the course instructor to determine whether instruction is needed? Answers to these questions are not clear, as there is rarely a systematic implementation of plagiarism prevention instruction. Another question that is becoming clearer is, Who is responsible for delivering the instruction? In recent years, librarians have been involved in the design and delivery of plagiarism avoidance instruction. A survey of a sample of librarians, conducted in 2010 by Gibson and Chester-Fangman,[27] found that 87 percent (530 of 608 respondents) believed that they had a role in plagiarism prevention. This is not surprising given that one of the outcomes in standard 5.2 in the Association of College and Research Libraries (ACRL) Information Literacy Competency Standards for Higher Education (2000) states that the information-literate individual "demonstrates an understanding of what constitutes plagiarism and does not represent work attributable to others as his/her own."[28] The ACRL has extended its commitment to teaching students to appropriately use information sources with their recent implementation of the ACRL Framework for Information Literacy for Higher Education. This framework, titled *Information Has Value*, addresses the need to "give credit to the original ideas of others through proper attribution and citation."[29]

Librarians support the delivery of plagiarism prevention instruction through workshops, one-shot library instruction sessions, tutorials, Web pages, and handouts.[30] *Teaching Information Literacy Threshold Concepts: Lesson Plans for Librarians* provides library instruction curriculum to address plagiarism-related issues.[31] One lesson plan focuses on strategies to assist the unintentional plagiarist by asking students to evaluate examples of plagiarism that are not clear-cut. In this lesson plan, students break into small groups and discuss a scenario to determine an acceptable course of action for a specific plagiarism violation. After discussing the scenario in the small groups, the entire class convenes to review the scenario and share highlights from small-group discussion. At the end of the session, students write a paragraph explaining their understanding of plagiarism.[32] Another method of instruction is to use nonacademic instances of plagiarism and ask students to discuss why the act was considered plagiarism and how it could have been avoided. The instruction session defines elements of plagiarism, including paraphrasing, quoting, and borrowing ideas.[33] Cara Bradley promotes using real-world examples in her book *Plagiarism Education and Prevention: A Subject-Driven, Case-Based Approach.*[34] She provides examples of plagiarism cases and discussion questions based on academic discipline. Bradley's real-world cases provide an opportunity for students to delve into the complex issues of plagiarism when viewed in the context of specific disciplines. A three-part student-centered approach employed by Moniz, Fine, and Bliss[35] starts by using small-group discussions where students brainstorm to come up with a definition of plagiarism. Then students review paraphrased passages and discuss whether these passages were correctly or incorrectly paraphrased. Finally, students participate in role-playing exercises in which one student is a professor confronting a student about a plagiarized paper and the other student assumes the role of the student justifying or denying the act.

Ideally, a comprehensive plan to implement plagiarism prevention instruction should exist at the institutional level or, at the very least, the departmental level. There are many instances where librarians collaborate with faculty and staff from academic support centers to develop a broadly disseminated plagiarism prevention curriculum. For example, at Boston College, a committee consisting of a librarian and faculty created an online tutorial addressing plagiarism prevention and academic integrity. All first-year students are required to complete an online tutorial and quiz. Some librarians have had success at the department level. Librarians, in conjunction with faculty from the Department of Computer Science at San Diego State University, developed a tutorial that was assigned to computer science majors taking their required technical writing course.[36] Librarians from Oakland University collaborated with staff from their Writing Center to revamp an online academic integrity tutorial. The tutorial consisted of six modules, and students received a certificate on completion. While the online tutorial was not a required, within four months of implementation, over 1,600 students had completed the course.[37]

Some course instructors do not provide plagiarism prevention instruction because they hold the perception that students learned how to avoid plagiarizing papers in high school. Given that an instructor is teaching students with diverse high school backgrounds, that perception is often faulty. However, some academic librarians recognize that this perception exists and are remedying it from two fronts. Librarians at Centenary College are not only providing plagiarism prevention instruction sessions in their institution but also reaching out to local high schools to offer workshops on academic integrity and plagiarism prevention to students.[38]

Many of these teaching strategies help address the issues associated with the unintentional plagiarist. The instruction sessions first define what plagiarism is and then discuss the importance of citation and paraphrasing correctly with some practice of these skills in the form of class exercises or assignments. Given the frequency of unintentional plagiarism cases,[39] educating students about the elements of scholarly writing is an important step in reducing the prevalence of plagiarism in the university setting.

Assignment Design

The design of an assignment can help reduce plagiarism tendencies in students. The instructor or the librarian, in collaboration with the instructor, can design an effective assignment that will make it more difficult to plagiarize the assignment. One strategy is to assign all students the same paper topic or provide a list of topics from which they can choose. By having students write on a limited number of topics, instructors are able to become familiar with the subject matter, making it easier to recognize repetitious phrases that may suggest nonoriginal thoughts.[40] Another strategy is to require specific components to the assignment. This could be a list of the types and number of sources to include in the bibliography or an infographic that illustrates a point in the paper or a personal experience.[41] Breaking the research paper into bite-size chunks can help those students who have time management issues. In this tactic, students are required to complete portions of the assignment across multiple deadlines to help prevent procrastination. To motivate students to invest time and effort into these assignment "chunks," instructors can make these assignments worth several points. For example, if an instructor broke a research assignment into three chunks and each chunk was worth several points, this assignment structure may minimize the perceived value of plagiarizing to students.[42] Another assignment chunk could include a graded peer review. This method has the additional benefit of improving student writing through the review–feedback–editing process.

Quality assignment design can help address the inclinations of the contextual and intentional plagiarists. If assignments are designed well, it is easier for the student to complete the assignment legitimately than to plagiarize. Breaking assignments into segments also assists those who have issues of time management because they do not have the opportunity to wait until the last minute to complete the assignment.

Codes of Conduct

Nearly all universities have a student code of conduct that outlines the expectations of students and potential penalties for violating the code. The student code of conduct addresses all behaviors expected from students during their tenure at the academic institution. A section usually relates to academic integrity. Codes of conduct have the potential to serve as a prevention strategy for plagiarism. The success is dependent on how faculty and administration apply the codes. Some instructors will embed the academic integrity section of the student codes into their syllabus. Some institutions have gone further and have had "swearing-in" ceremonies or developed professional oaths.[43] The code of conduct is meant not to serve as a scare tactic but rather to facilitate a conversation about the purpose of the university and why students are there. Each assignment is created to enhance student learning. For students to fully embrace the university experience, they should strive to complete the assignment honestly and to the best of their abilities.[44]

It is unlikely that students spend time reading through the student code of conduct during their free time. Many students are likely aware that plagiarism is wrong but may not be aware of the penalties for being caught. In some cases, students may not know that plagiarism is a violation of academic integrity. This may be especially true for some international students in cases where plagiarism is not a topic discussed at a university. International students may not know what plagiarism is. If they do know the concept, they may interpret the silence on the topic as a form of tacit acceptability.[45] The onus is on faculty and university administration to make students aware of what is expected of them. By embedding the code into the syllabus and having a discussion about academic integrity in the classroom, instructors are not only setting the expectation for the class but also leveling the playing field among students. Students cannot use the excuse of not knowing that plagiarism is a form of academic misconduct.

Honor codes in and of themselves are unlikely to prevent all forms of academic misconduct. Students intent on cheating and plagiarizing will likely continue to do so. However, honor codes may serve as an effective deterrent for those students who are on the cusp of cheating—as is often the case with the contextual plagiarist. If the honor code is consistently reinforced by appearing in the syllabus and class discussions and the submission of an honor pledge, then students who are tempted to plagiarize but know that it is wrong may be swayed from doing so.[46]

Detection Strategies

The second prong of plagiarism prevention is detection. As much as universities may invest in prevention strategies, plagiarism continues to exist in large part due to the intentional plagiarist, who is unreceptive to prevention techniques. Intentional plagiarists believe they have a better chance of getting away with plagiarizing a paper than of getting caught. An effective system of detection, followed by firm and consistent penalties for violations, may be a more successful deterrent to intentional plagiarists.

Many universities are investing in plagiarism detection software, such as Turnitin. Plagiarism detection software works well because it creates a databank of previous

students' papers and information available widely on the Web. Having a robust da-
tabase makes it easier to detect students' instances of plagiarism and is more efficient
than searching phrases through a search engine. Detection software should not serve
as the definitive source for identifying plagiarism. There are instances where plagiarism detection software will not recognize a case of plagiarism.[47] Ideally, instructors
would incorporate a couple of writing assignments into their curriculum. If they
become familiar with a student's writing style and see a paper that is significantly
different, it may send up a red flag. Even if a course does not have multiple writing
assignments, a careful reading of a student's paper will likely result in the professor
recognizing odd phrases or a lack of continuity or flow in the paper. Conversely,
plagiarism detection can also generate false-positive reports, suggesting that a student
plagiarized when in fact he or she did not.[48] Given that these systems are not fail-
safe, instructors need to review the report and carefully review students' papers to
determine whether a plagiarism detection software report is accurate.

Students and faculty have varying views on the use of plagiarism detection software. Some faculty view the university's purchase of plagiarism detection software as
a sign that they are committed to holding students accountable to the student code
of conduct.[49] Some students view these systems as a leveling of the playing field.
Understandably, honest students who do not plagiarize are often frustrated when
plagiarists do not get caught and then receive a better grade on a paper than they do.
They feel that having a system in place to catch plagiarists provides a sense of justice
and fairness.[50] Conversely, in the same study, several students thought that the use of
detection software was a clear statement from faculty and university administration
that they do not trust students to adhere to the code of conduct. They also viewed
the time to upload the paper and review the report to be a menial task with little
benefit.[51]

While it may appear that the only value to plagiarism detection software is to serve
in identifying intentionally plagiarized papers, it can also serve as a teaching tool for
students who are still in the process of learning how to cite and paraphrase properly.
When instructors enable students to access their common content reports, students
can submit their work early, see whether portions of their papers are plagiarized, and
make edits prior to submitting their final draft. For unintentional plagiarists, this
provides an opportunity for them to review the work they did and try to understand
why passages of their papers are considered to be plagiarized.[52]

PEAT

The teaching strategies, assignment design, and codes of conduct are important
tools that should be included in plagiarism prevention. These strategies can go far
in helping students who genuinely want to do honest work and succeed in becoming proficient writers. However, some of these techniques may not counteract the
intentional or contextual plagiarist. Moving forward in this discussion, we include

both intentional and contextual plagiarists in our use of *intentional plagiarism*. As we discussed above, although the justification for plagiarism differs for the intentional and contextual plagiarist, the *intention* of presenting the work of others as his or her own is a commonality between these two terms. These individuals likely know how to cite properly and paraphrase. The reason they do not is that they do not feel that plagiarism is wrong or they feel that the risks of getting caught are negligible. No amount of instruction on citing sources or proper paraphrasing will change that. Reviewing the code of conduct will not likely have an impact on these plagiarists because they do not accept the basic premise for the code, which is to come to the university to learn. Assignment design and plagiarism detection software may address the issue because plagiarizing becomes more difficult and the intentional plagiarist may not feel that the effort needed to plagiarize properly is worth the risk.

To prevent the intentional plagiarist from committing acts of plagiarism, there must be a change in one's perception about the ethicality of plagiarism. Plagiarism is often discussed as a moral and ethical issue. Trussell has described ways that librarians can collaborate with faculty (in this case, engineering faculty) to incorporate ethics into information literacy instruction,[53] which can help address criteria in a discipline's accreditation process. However, as instructors, we do not always present evidence that demonstrates that plagiarism is indeed a breach of ethics. More attention has been given to the ethical discussion surrounding academic conduct, and instructors are starting to incorporate aspects of ethics into plagiarism prevention instruction. For example, Cogdell and Aidulis developed a training program for graduate-level students in biomedical and life sciences with the outcome of presenting plagiarism as an unethical act using the following strategies:

• Providing written and verbal overviews of policies and student-signed honor pledges
• Improving assignment design
• Plagiarism prevention instruction
• Professional and research ethics workshop[54]

The first three points are consistent with strategies for plagiarism prevention outlined earlier in the chapter. The unique component is a four-hour workshop on the topic of ethics. Their workshop consisted of an overview of ethical decision making, focusing briefly on ethical theories and professional ethics. After reviewing theory and professional standards, the workshop shifted to case-based discussions in research ethics. The cases used in this workshop addressed topics including order of authorship, use of animals in experiments, and double publishing. The final portion of the workshop was a role-play scenario to practice skills around the implementation of a code of ethics.[55] The discussion scenarios and role-playing activity loosely touched on aspects of plagiarism but were focused primarily on other aspects of ethical research applicable to graduate research students.

Building off the work of Cogdell and Aidulis, we would like to offer a new approach, PEAT, which introduces plagiarism as a moral issue by couching it in ethical theory. The PEAT program is intended for postsecondary and college students. As reviewed earlier in this chapter, there are several strategies and efforts to prevent plagiarism targeted at the unintentional plagiarist. Although we recommend that PEAT be presented along with additional instruction in the area of plagiarism prevention skills, in this model, we do not duplicate these efforts. The PEAT program extends existing approaches to prevent plagiarism by focusing on the ethics surrounding plagiarism. In a PEAT approach, we ask students to apply ethical principles to a plagiarism scenario. After applying the principles, they need to determine if the action in the scenario was ethical. Our premise for this program of plagiarism prevention instruction is this: by clearly outlining why plagiarism is unethical using accepted ethical theories, we can shape student perceptions toward plagiarism and ultimately decrease the incidence of student plagiarism in academia.

PEAT is intended to serve as a prevention model for intentional plagiarists. As mentioned earlier, these individuals plagiarize because they do not think plagiarism is wrong or they feel that they will not get caught. With this model, we are attempting to alter these perceptions toward plagiarism. If students logically work through a scenario and for each ethical theory applied reach the same conclusion (plagiarism is unethical), then their attitude about plagiarism may begin to shift.

Again, the PEAT program is not meant to replace the teaching strategies, assignment design, and plagiarism detection software methods outlined earlier in this chapter. The methods are crucial in reducing unintentional plagiarism. Rather, PEAT is an approach that can be used to complement these strategies by offering a critical evaluation of plagiarism from an ethical perspective. Part II of this book provides detailed information about how you can implement PEAT during your next plagiarism prevention instruction session.

NOTES

1. Tricia Bertram Gallant, "Twenty-First Century Forces Shaping Academic Integrity," *ASHE Higher Education Report* 33, no. 5 (2008): 65–67, doi:10.1002/aehe.3305.

2. Angela D. Miller, Tamera B. Murdock, Eric M. Anderman, and Amy L. Poindexter, "Who Are All the Cheaters? Characteristics of Academically Dishonest Students," in *Psychology of Academic Cheating*, ed. Eric M. Anderman and Tamera B. Murdock (Burlington, MA: Elsevier Academic Press, 2007), 29.

3. Stephen F. Davis, Patrick F. Drinan, and Tricia Bertram Gallant, *Cheating in School: What We Know and What We Can Do* (Malden, MA: Wiley-Blackwell, 2009), 73.

4. Ibid., 78–79.

5. Gregory Schraw, Lori Olafson, Fred Kuch, Trish Lehman, Stephen Lehman, and Matthew T. McCrudden, "Interest and Academic Cheating," in Anderman and Murdock, *Psychology of Academic Cheating*, 70.

6. Davis et al., *Cheating in School*, 79.

7. Schraw et al., "Interest and Academic Cheating," 67–68; Davis et al., *Cheating in School*, 79.

8. Schraw et al., "Interest and Academic Cheating," 69.

9. Deone Zell, "The Market-Driven Business School: Has the Pendulum Swung Too Far?," *Journal of Management Inquiry* 10, no. 4 (2001): 330–32.

10. Barry Gilmore, *Plagiarism: Why It Happens, How to Prevent It* (Portsmouth, NH: Heinemann, 2008), 54.

11. Tracy Bretag and Saadia Mahmud, "A Model for Determining Student Plagiarism: Electronic Detection and Academic Judgement," *Journal of University Teaching and Learning Practice* 6, no. 1 (2009): 52, http://ro.uow.edu.au/cgi/viewcontent.cgi?article=1076&context=jutlp; James M. Lang, *Cheating Lessons: Learning from Academic Dishonesty* (Cambridge, MA: Harvard University Press, 2013), 213–15.

12. Davis et al., *Cheating in School*, 156–60.

13. Richard Perez-Pena, "Students Disciplined in Harvard Scandal," *New York Times*, February 1, 2013, http://www.nytimes.com/2013/02/02/education/harvard-forced-dozens-to-leave-in-cheating-scandal.html.

14. Davis et al., *Cheating in School*, 156–57.

15. Ibid., 158.

16. Ibid., 159.

17. Ibid.

18. Erika Lofstrom and Paulina Kupila, "The Instructional Challenges of Student Plagiarism," *Journal of Academic Ethics* 11, no. 3 (2013): 236, http://link.springer.com/article/10.1007 percent2Fs10805-013-9181-z.

19. Ibid., 273.

20. John Walker, "Student Plagiarism in Universities: What Are We Doing about It?," *Higher Education Research and Development* 17, no. 1 (1998): 103, http://dx.doi.org/10.1080/0729436980170105.

21. Judith Gullifer and Graham A. Tyson, "Exploring University Students' Perceptions of Plagiarism: A Focus Group Study," *Studies in Higher Education* 35, no. 4 (2010): 469–70, http://dx.doi.org/10.1080/03075070903096508; Gilmore, *Plagiarism*, 48.

22. Lofstrom and Kupila, "The Instructional Challenges of Student Plagiarism," 236.

23. Ibid.

24. Walker, "Student Plagiarism in Universities," 102–3.

25. Lofstrom and Kupila, "The Instructional Challenges of Student Plagiarism," 236.

26. U.S. Department of Education, National Center for Education Statistics, *The Condition of Education 2015* (NCES 2015-144), Employment Rates and Unemployment Rates by Educational Attainment.

27. Nancy Snyder Gibson and Christina Chester-Fangman, "The Librarian's Role in Combating Plagiarism," *Reference Services Review* 39, no. 1 (2011): 138, http://dx.doi.org/10.1108/00907321111108169.

28. Association of College and Research Libraries, "Information Literacy Competency Standards for Higher Education," 2000, http://www.ala.org/acrl/standards/informationliteracycompetency, accessed January 3, 2016.

29. Association of College and Research Libraries, "Framework for Information Literacy for Higher Education," 2015, 6, accessed January 3, 2016, http://www.ala.org/acrl/sites/ala.org.acrl/files/content/issues/infolit/Framework_ILHE.pdf, accessed January 3, 2016.

30. Gibson and Chester-Fangman, "The Librarian's Role in Combating Plagiarism," 143.

31. Smita Avasthi, "Gray Areas in Plagiarism Cases," in *Teaching Information Literacy Threshold Concepts: Lesson Plans for Librarians*, ed. Patricia Bravender, Hazel McClure, and Gayle Schaub (Chicago: Association of College and Research Libraries, 2015), 150–51; Patricia Bravender and Gayle Schaub, "Recognizing Plagiarism," in *Teaching Information Literacy Threshold Concepts: Lesson Plans for Librarians, ed. Patricia Bravender*, Hazel McClure, and Gayle Schaub (Chicago: Association of College and Research Libraries, 2015), 146–76.

32. Avasthi, "Gray Areas," 150–51.

33. Bravender and Schaub, "Recognizing Plagiarism," 164.

34. Cara Bradley, *Plagiarism Education and Prevention: A Subject-Driven, Case-Based Approach* (Oxford: Chandos, 2011).

35. Richard Moniz, Joyce Fine, and Leonard Bliss, "The Effectiveness of Direct-Instruction and Student-Centered Teaching Methods on Students' Functional Understanding of Plagiarism," *College and Undergraduate Libraries* 15, no. 3 (2008): 266–67, http://www.tandfonline.com/doi/pdf/10.1080/10691310802258174.

36. Pamela A. Jackson, "Plagiarism Instruction Online: Assessing Undergraduate Students' Ability to Avoid Plagiarism," *College and Research Libraries* 67, no. 5 (2006): 422, http://crl.acrl.org/content/67/5/418.full.pdf.

37. Katie Greer, Stephanie Swanberg, Mariela Hristova, Anne T. Switzer, Dominique Daniel, and Sherry Wynn Perdue, "Beyond the Web Tutorial: Development and Implementation of an Online, Self-Directed Academic Integrity Course at Oakland University," *Journal of Academic Librarianship* 38, no. 5 (2012): 251–58, http://www.sciencedirect.com/science/article/pii/S0099133312001127.

38. Christy Wrenn and Kristi Kohl, "Ensuring Academic Integrity through Community and Campus Outreach," *Codex: The Journal of the Louisiana Chapter of the ACR* 2, no. 1 (2012): 58–70, http://journal.acrlla.org/index.php/codex/article/view/64/123.

39. Angela L. Walker, "Preventing Unintentional Plagiarism: A Method for Strengthening Paraphrasing Skills," *Journal of Instructional Psychology* 35, no. 4 (2008): 388.

40. Robert A. Harris, *The Plagiarism Handbook: Strategies for Preventing, Detecting, and Dealing with Plagiarism* (Los Angeles: Pyrczak Publishing, 2001), 44–45; Lynn D. Lampert, *Combating Student Plagiarism: An Academic Librarian's Guide* (Oxford, England: Chandos, 2008), 124.

41. Harris, *The Plagiarism Handbook*, 49–50; Lampert, *Combating Student Plagiarism*, 124; Gilmore, *Plagiarism*, 102.

42. Harris, *The Plagiarism Handbook*, 51–52; Lampert, *Combating Student Plagiarism*, 124; Gilmore, *Plagiarism*, 101.

43. Sally Sledge and Pam Pringle, "Assessing Honor Code Effectiveness: Results of a Multipronged Approach from a Five Year Study," *Research and Practice in Assessment* 5 (Winter 2010): 5, http://www.rpajournal.com/dev/wp-content/uploads/2012/05/A15.pdf.

44. Lofstrom and Kupila, "The Instructional Challenges of Student Plagiarism," 240.

45. Diane Pecorari, *Teaching to Avoid Plagiarism: How to Promote Good Source Use* (New York: Open University Press, 2013), 109.

46. Gilmore, *Plagiarism*, 130–31.

47. Pecorari, *Teaching to Avoid Plagiarism*, 50.

48. Bretag and Mahmud, "A Model for Determining Student Plagiarism," 54; Davis et al., *Cheating in School*, 112.

49. Lampert, *Combating Student Plagiarism*, 134.

50. Lofstrom and Kupila, "The Instructional Challenges of Student Plagiarism," 239.

51. Ibid.

52. Ibid., 238.

53. Alice Trussell, "Librarians and Engineering Faculty: Partnership Opportunities in Information Literacy and Ethics Instruction," 25th IATUL Conference, Krakow, Poland, June 2004, http://www.iatul.org/doclibrary/public/Conf_Proceedings/2004/Alice20Trussell.pdf.

54. Barbara Cogdell and Dorothy Aidulis, "Dealing with Plagiarism as an Ethical Issue," in *Student Plagiarism in an Online World: Problems and Solutions*, ed. Tim S. Roberts (Hershey, PA: Information Science Reference, 2008), 42.

55. Ibid., 51–52.

2

Thinking through the Ethics of Plagiarism

A Crash Course

Ethics has long been a topic of interest across multiple disciplines. The question of what is right or wrong and what drives us to commit right or wrong acts has been considered by philosophers and religious figures throughout history. In recent years, ethics has arisen as a key concern in contemporary society as highly publicized incidents of unethical conduct plague business practices with great, far-reaching impact. Most of us have heard of Enron, WorldCom, Bernie Madoff, and Lehman Brothers. But we didn't consider the ethical implications of their actions until *after* these large scandals had occurred. Each of these frauds stimulates outrage in the media. Following these events, the public frequently turns to institutions of higher education to help students consider ethics *before* committing behavior that may lead to public scandals and fraud. Business schools and institutions of higher education have responded to this challenge by endeavoring to train students to be more ethical employees in their future jobs. This has led to a proliferation of ethics research and training in the past three decades as well as a greater awareness of ethical and unethical behavior across a range of contexts.

Longitudinal research indicates high and increasing levels of academic dishonesty among students ranging from 52 to 90 percent participation in cheating.[1] Research also has found that cheating is widespread at all levels of schooling and increases from primary to secondary and postsecondary schools.[2] Further studies have established that unethical behavior in college leads to unethical behavior in work contexts.[3] This suggests that university educators have a challenging but critical role to play in the improvement of ethical behavior in both academic and workplace contexts. Given the pattern of increased cheating at postsecondary schools as well as the perception by university presidents that student plagiarism has increased at their institutions,[4] a Plagiarism and Ethics Awareness Training (PEAT) program stands to make an important contribution to the effort to produce more ethical students and future employees.

In this chapter, we provide a general overview of ethics research to date, placing particular emphasis on business ethics research and models, theories, and philosophies that are relevant to our discussion of PEAT programs. We explore the application of these ethics concepts in chapter 4. In this chapter, we examine the theoretical origins of these concepts. For the purposes of this discussion, we use the terms *ethics* and *morality* (including their variant forms) interchangeably.

RESEARCH ORIGINS OF ETHICS

Research in ethics originated in the domains of philosophy and political science where individuals such as Kant and Aristotle proposed moral ideologies (which are sometimes referred to as ethical *values* or *standards* in business ethics textbooks) to guide individuals in their deliberations of ethical dilemmas. Kant is credited with *deontology*, which essentially posits that we behave ethically when we conform to universal moral rules.[5] Aristotle offered a more practical view of ethics when he asserts that an individual can *become* moral through his or her upbringing as well as through practice.[6] Modern-day business ethics stems from research in psychology. Prior to the 1950s, this research centered on social influences that shaped how individuals developed morally.[7] In a social influence approach,[8] ethical actions are socialized within individuals by their cultural surroundings. An individual looks to his or her surroundings to determine a culturally sanctioned response to an ethical dilemma. Eventually, these culturally sanctioned responses become internalized within the individual.[9]

In the 1950s, psychologists Piaget and Kohlberg[10] each engaged in research exploring the cognitive processes of an individual apart from social or cultural influences. This started a trend that has dominated the past four decades in ethics research exploring moral judgment or ethical decision making. In the 1970s, James Rest, a student of Kohlberg's, developed a four-part model of morality that included moral judgment as well as other individual and situational factors that precede, interact with, or follow judgment in the process of morality.[11] This model emphasizes what must happen cognitively and emotionally as well as situationally in order for individuals to behave ethically, which is the ultimate objective of moral deliberation.[12] Rest's model of morality has had a significant impact on business ethics research from the late 1970s through the start of this millennium.[13]

Rest's model requires individuals to focus on the outcome of their actions while deliberating and devising a plan to overcome multiple internal and external obstacles.[14] The first component of this model is *moral sensitivity*. Moral sensitivity requires individuals to identify alternative responses to an ethical dilemma and consider the potential impact of their responses on others. For example, Sara finds a wallet in the street and while deliberating what to do with it considers how her actions might impact the owner of the wallet, his family members, and his ability to attend to financial obligations. The second component is *moral judgment*, where individuals choose which alternative, identified in component 1, is the "right" response in the given situation. Sara might engage in moral judgment by considering alternative actions—leaving the wallet on the ground, pocketing the money but turning the wallet in to a lost and found, or returning the wallet and its contents to the owner—and decide that returning the wallet and its contents to the owner is the most ethical alternative. The third component, *moral motivation*, entails individuals prioritizing moral values over other values in a particular ethical dilemma. Sara must decide that returning the wallet to the owner is more valuable to her than using the money she finds in the wallet to pay her rent this month. The fourth component of this model is *moral character*. An individual with moral character is able to convert his or her behavioral intentions, which are formed in component 3, into ethical behaviors. Even after prioritizing doing the right thing over paying rent, Sara might not actually follow through with the ethical behavior of returning the wallet to its owner—a number of events could cause Sara to waver. For example, perhaps she gets a parking ticket before she can return the wallet and decides to use the money to pay the ticket, or perhaps she tries to return the wallet but after weeks of not hearing back from the owner decides to spend the money. Although ethical behavior is the culmination of this model, several personal and situational factors can prevent ethical behavior from taking place.[15]

Rest's model allows us to consider how a student may go astray when deliberating whether to plagiarize. For example, Jane may consider the negative outcomes of plagiarism should she get caught. Further, she may consider that plagiarizing her work will only exacerbate difficulties writing a quality research paper in future classes or when she is employed. Jane might realize that plagiarizing her paper may alter the grade distribution of this assignment, and this may impact her fellow classmates. Finally, she may realize that committing plagiarism may have a negative impact on her instructor and administrative officials at the university, particularly if she's caught. This may lead Jane to determine that the "right" decision if to not plagiarize her research paper. At this point in her moral deliberation, Jane seems to have successfully engaged in components 1 and 2 of Rest's model. However, as she advances to component 3, Jane may realize that her grade-point average stands to suffer if she does not achieve a superior grade on this research paper. As a result, she may prioritize maintaining her grade-point average over the moral value of "doing the right thing," and this leads Jane to commit plagiarism in component 4 of Rest's model. Although she identified alternative actions, considered their impact on others, and made a moral judgment, Jane lacked the moral motivation and moral character to follow through with ethical behavior in this situation.

While this is a hypothetical scenario in an academic context, this example can be applied to the business world. One might consider that Bernie Madoff, responsible for one of the largest financial frauds in U.S. history,[16] was likely aware of the potential impact of his fraudulent actions on others and had made a judgment of the ethical, "right" thing to do. However, like Jane in the above scenario, Madoff lacked the moral motivation and moral character to follow through with the ethically "right" behavior, and this led to his investors losing $10 to $17 billion.[17]

KEY CONCEPTS AND MODELS

Rest's model encompasses cognitive processes, values, personality traits, and situational factors that may influence moral deliberation. These foundations are central concepts and models that underlie the PEAT program. Here we introduce stakeholder theory, ethical climates, research background for theoretical and practical criteria guiding ethical decisions, and Mary Gentile's Giving Voice to Values framework. These concepts and models lay the foundation for the pedagogical and curricular design discussed in chapters 3 and 4.

Stakeholder Theory

As emphasized in component 1 of Rest's model of morality, an important step in ethical decision making is to identify and consider the interests and welfare of stakeholders in any given ethical dilemma.[18] Argondoña[19] proposed that the foundational premise of stakeholder theory is the goal of the *common good*, which emphasizes the well-being of society and all of its members, or stakeholders. According to Post, Lawrence, and Weber, stakeholders "are those people and groups that affect, or can be affected by, an organization's decisions, policies, and operations."[20] By conducting a thorough stakeholder analysis, decision makers can counter the rationalization that an unethical action is a "victimless crime."

Post and colleagues[21] suggest that the number of stakeholders that are relevant to a given decision can vary, as can the interests held by stakeholders. While some stakeholders share in the positive outcomes gained by a decision maker, others might assume the risks of a given decision.[22] When conducting a stakeholder analysis in an ethical dilemma, it may be helpful to delineate *primary* and *secondary* stakeholders. In the context of a business, primary stakeholders are those parties directly involved in the business's mission of delivering products or services for its customer base, where secondary stakeholders include parties who display an interest in the business's actions.[23]

When we extrapolate the definition of primary stakeholders to the case of a student confronted with the decision whether to plagiarize in an assignment, primary stakeholders would include parties such as the student him- or herself as well as the student's classmates, instructors, and the author(s) of the work the student might plagiarize (this is further explored in chapter 4). For a student considering whether to plagiarize an assignment, secondary stakeholders are parties who are directly *or* indirectly impacted by this decision.[24] This could include university administrators, such as the dean of students, who may be responsible for reviewing violations of the student conduct code; future employers, who seek to hire ethical employees; the media, who may publicize a pattern of unethical student activities at the university; and the general public, who will form positive or negative opinions of the university based on aggregate student behaviors.[25] Post and colleagues assert that to make a good decision, individuals must consider "the effects of those decisions—pro and con—on the people and interests [primary *and* secondary stakeholders] that are affected."[26]

Ethical Climate Research

An organization's ethical climate also can influence the decision-making processes and behavior of individuals. An *ethical climate* describes how members of an organization "typically make decisions concerning various 'events, practices, and procedures' requiring ethical criteria."[27] An ethical work climate indicates that an organization's norms toward ethical behavior are entrenched within the organizational culture.[28] Several studies have found examined culture and climate as key influences on ethical decision processes.[29] An ethical climate or culture may stem from a particular moral philosophy or alternate ethical structure, such as the law.[30] Codes of ethics as well as corresponding rewards and sanctions may also shape an ethical climate. Research suggests that ethics codes increase individual sensitivity to ethical issues and an awareness of ethical transgressions in an organization.[31] However, for ethics codes to be effective, they must be combined with appropriate actions to enforce these codes.[32]

In the context of a student deliberating whether to plagiarize, an ethical climate is in part shaped by the university's stated academic code of conduct and its norms for enforcing this code. The enforcement of sanctions for violations of a student conduct code has been found to decrease the incidence of cheating.[33] However, research also shows that faculty are largely charged with this enforcement and may find this task unrewarding and sometimes punitive.[34] This is supported by research that has found that although 79 percent of faculty reported catching a student in the act of cheating, only 9 percent reported reprimanding a student for cheating.[35] Additional research has found that when instructors neglect their monitoring responsibilities, cheating among students increases.[36]

An effective PEAT program may result in a shift of some of the responsibility for enforcement of the student conduct code from faculty members to the students. By providing students with the tools to avoid plagiarism as well as the understanding of the ethics of plagiarism and how this relates to university expectations for ethical student conduct, the PEAT program can provide students with the skills and compelling interest to comply with the university's academic conduct code, and in the aggregate, this can increase the ethical *culture* of the institution. The communication of university expectations for student behavior is further explored in chapters 3 and 4.

Theoretical Criteria

Recognizing the multifaceted qualities of the ethical decision-making process in business ethics, Reidenbach and Robin[37] conceived of the Multidimensional Ethics

Scale (MES) grounded on a three-factor view of ethical judgment. They derived the MES from normative moral philosophies. In other words, this scale captures from respondents what they think *should be done* more than what they think actually *is done* when it comes to ethical judgment.[38] Their refinement of this scale in 1990 resulted in eight items that represent three moral philosophies: moral equity, relativism, and contractualism. This scale has been widely used across multiple disciplines, including accounting, management, and marketing disciplines of business, as well as in the context of academic honesty.[39] Further, it has been tested on multiple populations, including a diverse range of professions.[40]

Reidenbach and Robin[41] conceive of *moral equity* broadly to include elements of deontology (moral rightness) and justice. They claim that this dimension encompasses essential guidance for appraising the ethical substance of situations. When drawing on this dimension, individuals evaluate decisions on the basis of their "fairness, justice, goodness and rightness" as well as their likelihood to be acceptable to family members.[42] The authors discuss how family members instill within us ideals of fairness, justice, and rightness at an early age. Thus, when we evaluate ethical content later in life, we invoke thoughts and memories of our influential moral teachers in this process.

Relativism represents the "guidelines, requirements, and parameters inherent in the social/cultural system."[43] This dimension acknowledges the important influence of social and cultural systems on our ethical beliefs and decision-making processes. This requires individuals to have accrued a sufficient number of social interactions to develop a functional understanding of social norms pertaining to the ethical content of a given situation. Further, this dimension can account for cultural variation in assessing the ethical content of various situations.

The third dimension of MES is *contractualism*. Reidenbach and Robin[44] describe contractualism as a wholly deontological factor that addresses ideals such as responsibility, duty, and adhering to rules. This dimension is rooted in the ideal of social contracts where an implicit or explicit exchange exists between parties that obligates one party to provide a good or perform an action in trade for something of value from the other party. Underlying the obligation of this contract is the notion of ethics—the parties are morally bound by this contract, and violations of this contract are deemed to be unethical.[45]

In the PEAT program, we base our theoretical criteria for ethical deliberation on these three dimensions and ask students, when considering plagiarism and its ethical ramifications, to consider three MES items, each representing its own dimension:

1. Was the action fair? (moral equity)
2. Is the action culturally acceptable? (relativism)
3. Does the action violate an unwritten contract? (contractualism)

These theoretical criteria are discussed in chapters 4 and 5. In chapter 7, we revisit the MES as an assessment tool in evaluating level 2 outcomes of the PEAT program.

Practical Criteria

Much business ethics instruction involves the review of numerous moral philosophies or ethical standards. This can be both complex and overwhelming for business professionals and students and may trigger "ethics fatigue."[46] This may increase decision-making time and decrease the likelihood that this information will be used or used correctly when individuals confront ethical situations.[47] In the PEAT program, we identify the following practical criteria to support students to make timely ethical decisions:

1. Does the action fall within the usual standards? (organizational and professional ethics)
2. Would I feel comfortable viewing this action on the front page of the newspaper? (front-page-of-the-newspaper test)
3. Would I be willing to share this action with family and friends? (moral equity)

When we consider whether an action falls within the *usual standards*, it invokes our previous theoretical discussion of *relativism*. The usual standards broadly represent social and cultural norms, and when we think of these standards in a workplace ethical dilemma, the usual standards tend to be depicted by a professional code of ethics within an organization or professional membership group. A profession is a group of occupations that share a clear set of characteristics,[48] which may include training requirements, a certifying body, and similar stakeholder groups.[49] Frankel[50] delineates eight possible functions of a professional code: (1) provide guidance for individuals facing new situations, (2) provide a foundation for public expectations of the profession, (3) establish a common purpose within the organization, (4) boost the profession's reputation and public confidence, (5) uphold deep-seated professional values, (6) prevent unethical behavior by outlining potential consequences and by encouraging reporting behaviors, (7) offer support for those facing pressures in ethical dilemmas, and (8) serve as a mechanism to settle disputes within the profession. A university code of conduct may function as a professional code for students who are considering plagiarism in an academic context. Research suggests, however, that the code must be functional, not ceremonial, and salient to organizational members if it will effectively deter unethical behavior.[51]

The front-page-of-the-newspaper test originates in a quote by Warren Buffet when he assumed leadership at Salomon Brothers during a time when the company admitted to violations of bidding rules in the Treasury securities markets.[52] When he addressed employees of the company at this tumultuous time, he emphasized moving forward with a keen sense of ethics guiding their actions:

> Contemplating any business act, an employee should ask himself whether he would be willing to see it immediately described by an informed and critical reporter on the front page of his local paper, there to be read by his spouse, children, and friends. At Salomon, we simply want no part of any activities that pass legal tests but that we, as citizens, would find offensive.[53]

This quote has led to a widely used practical guide for ethical decision making in business. It is rooted in deontology in that if your chosen action is *morally correct*, you are willing to see it communicated in a public medium.

When you consider whether you are willing to communicate your ethical responses to your loved ones, you activate memories of your role models who helped you develop morally through your childhood and young adult life. As we discussed in theoretical criteria, moral equity involves fairness, justice, and rightness, and, more often than not, our family members instill these values within us. Asking an individual to communicate an unethical action to his or her family would likely constitute a shaming experience to many decision makers.

Whistle-Blowing Perspectives

The theories reviewed above focus on the decision maker as the potential transgressor in ethical situations. Whistle-blowing research looks at the role of observers in responding to and preventing future unethical actions. A whistle-blower is a current or former member of an organization that reports "illegal, immoral, or illegitimate practices under the control of their employers, to persons or organizations that may be able to effect action."[54] A college student who observes plagiarism in his or her class must decide whether to report this behavior. Whistle-blower research may illuminate the processes that this student undergoes when considering whether to report plagiarism in academic contexts. In their examination of whistle-blowers, Gundlach, Douglas, and Martinko[55] identify four theoretical foundations as they relate to whistle-blowers. These include power, justice, prosocial, and attribution perspectives on whistle-blower situations.

A power perspective of whistle-blowing examines the actions that wrongdoers may take to discourage others from reporting their unethical behavior.[56] If wrongdoers have more power than the would-be whistle-blowers, they may be more effective in preventing the reporting of their transgressions. Power can manifest in a variety of ways in an academic context. For example, a plagiarizer may have considerable referent power (social influence, which can manifest as popularity) in the social landscape of a university. A plagiarizer may use this power to dissuade or intimidate a potential whistle-blowing classmate.

A justice theory view of whistle-blowing emphasizes how individuals perceive and react to unethical behavior, including what actions they might take to resolve the perceived injustices stemming from observed unethical behavior.[57] When a student observes another who has plagiarized, this may trigger a response where he or she centers on the inequity resulting from plagiarism behavior. In this case, blowing the whistle and reporting plagiarism is his or her attempt to restore justice in this academic situation.

In a prosocial perspective of whistle-blowing, this reporting behavior is a compassionate action that individuals perform to uphold the good of society.[58] A student's cognitive moral development[59] as well as his or her commitment to the organization[60] may impact how prosocially motivated he or she is, and this will impact his or her whistle-blowing decision in a plagiarism situation. For example, if Joe has a low level of moral development and most of his actions depend on his perception of rewards or punishments that may stem from behavioral alternatives, he may choose to not report plagiarism for a low-stakes writing assignment at a school where plagiarism is generally dismissed as a minor infraction of school rules. However, if Joe is deeply committed to his university and feels compelled to support the school in upholding its student conduct code, he may be more compelled to view any infractions against this code as threats to the university, and therefore he will be more likely to report observed plagiarism.

An attribution theory view of whistle-blowing analyzes the reason why the event occurred. A potential whistle-blower will try to understand what led the perpetrator to conduct the unethical action before he or she decides whether to report the activity.[61] For example, if Jane learns that Joe plagiarized a class paper but overhears him talking about how he has been working 50 hours a week at his job so he can pay for his brother's medical bills, then Jane may feel empathy, assign an external attribution for the behavior (Joe's difficult situation led to his plagiarism behavior), and be less-inclined to report his infraction. However, if Jane hears Joe talking about how he plagiarized the paper so he could attend a party, then she may assign an internal attribution for the behavior (Joe prioritized social activities over academic and therefore chose to plagiarize), and may be more likely to be a whistle-blower in this situation.

Giving Voice to Values

The final foundational concept we draw on in the PEAT program is the Giving Voice to Values (GVV) framework.[62] Mary Gentile developed this framework after years of teaching business ethics and questioning the effectiveness of how she was teaching it, saying that "sometimes all they [students] learn is how to frame the case to justify virtually any position, no matter how cynical or self-serving."[63] The GVV framework shifts the ethical process from one where we evaluate the rightness of a decision or action to one where we determine how to respond when we know something unethical has happened. Recalling Rest's[64] four-component model of morality, this framework helps decision makers move from moral judgment to moral behavior by emphasizing the values conflict inherent in ethical dilemmas.

Gentile uses her GVV framework to challenge common excuses for silently allowing unethical behavior to take place. These excuses include "it's standard practice[,] it's not my responsibility[, and] I want to be loyal."[65] These are the same kinds of rationalizations a student might use to justify plagiarizing a research assignment or not reporting plagiarism committed by a classmate. In the GVV framework, we are encouraged to prioritize ethical values and to carefully plan a response to unethical behavior or unethical pressures that is consistent with these values.

Using the GVV framework in a plagiarism situation, consider Janet, who feels pressure to plagiarize a research assignment. Janet has taken on too many courses this semester while balancing a part-time job. Furthermore, her scholarship requires her to maintain a 3.5 grade-point average. If she does poorly on this research assignment, her scholarship will be in jeopardy. If Janet uses the GVV framework, she recognizes her moral situation and knows that the ethical thing to do is to *not* plagiarize. The challenge lies in how to connect what she knows is right with her behavior. The GVV framework would advocate that Janet consider her core values and the values that resonate in this particular situation. Janet may value being an ethical person and an ethical student. These values may appear to conflict with her academic scholarship, which she also values for different reasons. In spite of this conflict of values, Janet still has a choice, and she can choose to prioritize her core values over the situational values stemming from this particular situation. Often, an unethical situation is presented as an either/or choice: *either you plagiarize your research paper, or you lose your scholarship*. By examining her choices more carefully, Janet can reframe her ethical situation and discover alternate responses that may be more consistent with her core values.

Moreover, in this process, Janet can realize that this dilemma of whether to plagiarize is a normal values conflict that she will encounter repeatedly through her academic and professional careers. Ethical situations are not aberrations but regular occurrences in our daily lives.[66] This normalization of ethical situations can help Janet view this plagiarism decision less emotionally and more rationally so that she can be more effective in this type of situation. The GVV framework also encourages Janet to find strength in her current circumstances. She is a college student who works part-time, depends on her academic scholarship, and has registered for too many courses this semester. Rather than framing this situation as one filled with constraints leading Janet to plagiarize, she can frame her situation as one filled with choices. For example, Janet can reduce her work hours, as she is smart and can apply for additional academic scholarships, or she can choose to reduce her course load so that she has more time to invest in her research paper and feels less pressure to plagiarize.

NOTES

1. Randy L. Genereux and Beverly A. McLeod, "Circumstances Surrounding Cheating: A Questionnaire Study of College Students," *Research in Higher Education* 36, no. 6 (1995): 687–704, doi:10.1007/BF02208251; Melody A. Graham, Jacquelyn Monday, K. O'Brien, and S. Steffen, "Cheating at Small Colleges: An Examination of Student and Faculty Attitudes and Behaviors," *Journal of College Student Development* 35, no. 4 (1994): 255–60; Mindy Chaky Lester and George M. Diekhoff, "A Comparison of Traditional and Internet Cheaters," *Journal of College Student Development* 43, no. 6 (2002): 906–11; Donald L. McCabe and William J. Bowers, "The Relationship between Student Cheating and College Fraternity or Sorority Membership," *NASPA Journal* 46, no.4 (2009): 573–86, http://www.tandfonline.com/doi/pdf/10.2202/1949-6605.5032; Michael Vandehay, George Diekhoff, and Emily LaBeff, "College Cheating: A Twenty-Year Follow-Up and the Addition of an Honor Code," *Journal of College Student Development* 48, no. 4 (2007): 468–80, doi:10.1353/csd.2007.0043;

Paul R. Vowell and Jieming Chen, "Predicting Academic Misconduct: A Comparative Test of Four Sociological Explanations," *Sociological Inquiry* 74, no. 2 (2004): 226–49, doi:10.1111/j.1475-682X.2004.00088.x.

2. Eric M. Anderman, Tripp Griesinger, and Gloria Westerfield, "Motivation and Cheating during Early Adolescence," *Journal of Educational Psychology* 90, no. 1 (1998): 84–93, https://www.uky.edu/Centers/HIV/Eric%20Articles/Anderman%20et%20al.%201998.pdf; Marisa Luisa Farnese, Carlo Tramontano, Roberta Fida, and Marinella Paciello, "Cheating Behavior in Academic Context: Does Academic Moral Disengagement Matter?," *Procedia—Social and Behavioral Sciences* 29 (2011): 356–65, doi:10.1016/j.sbspro.2011.11.250; Lene Arnett Jensen, Jeffrey Jensen Arnett, S. Shirley Feldman, and Elizabeth Cauffman, "It's Wrong but Everybody Does It: Academic Dishonesty among High School and College Students," *Contemporary Educational Psychology* 27, no. 2 (2002): 209–28, doi:10.1006/ceps.2001.1088.

3. Sarath Nonis and Cathy Owens Swift, "An Examination of the Relationship between Academic Dishonesty and Workplace Dishonesty: A Multicampus Investigation," *Journal of Education for Business* 77, no. 2 (2001): 69–77; Randi L. Sims, "The Relationship between Academic Dishonesty and Unethical Business Practices," *Journal of Education for Business* 68, no. 4 (1993): 207–11.

4. Kim Parker, Amanda Lenhart, and Kathleen Moore, "The Digital Revolution and Higher Education: College Presidents, Public Differ on Value of Online Learning," 2011, http://www.pewinternet.org/files/old-media//Files/Reports/2011/PIP-Online-Learning.pdf.

5. S. Kagan, "Kantianism for Consequentialists," in *Groundwork for the Metaphysics of Morals with Essays by J. B. Schneewind, M. Baron, S. Kagan, and A. Wood*, ed. Allen Wood, (New Haven, CT: Yale University Press, 2002), 140.

6. Aristotle and Martin Ostwald, *Nicomachean Ethics* (Indianapolis: Bobbs-Merrill, 1962).

7. James R. Rest and Darcia Narváez, *Moral Development in the Professions: Psychology and Applied Ethics* (Hillsdale, NJ: Lawrence Erlbaum Associates, 1994).

8. Stephen M. Pittel and Gerald A. Mendelsohn, "Measurement of Moral Values: A Review and Critique," *Psychological Bulletin* 66, no. 1 (1966): 22–35, http://dx.doi.org/10.1037/h0023425.

9. Rest and Narváez, *Moral Development in the Professions*.

10. Jean Piaget, *The Moral Judgment of the Child*, trans. Marjorie Gabain (New York: Free Press, 1965); Lawrence Kohlberg, "Stage and Sequence: The Cognitive-Developmental Approach to Socialization," in *Handbook of Socialization Theory and Research*, ed. David A. Goslin (Chicago: Rand McNally, 1969), 347–480; Lawrence Kohlberg, "From Is to Ought: How to Commit the Naturalistic Fallacy and Get Away with It in the Study of Moral Development," in *Cognitive Development and Epistemology*, ed. Theodore Mischel (New York: Academic Press, 1971), 151–236.

11. James R. Rest, *Development in Judging Moral Issues* (Minneapolis: University of Minnesota Press, 1979).

12. James R. Rest, *Moral Development* (New York: Praeger, 1986).

13. Thomas M. Jones, "Ethical Decision Making by Individuals in Organizations: An Issue-Contingent Model," *Academy of Management Review* 16, no. 2 (1991): 366–95, http://www.jstor.org/stable/258867; Jana L. Craft, "A Review of the Empirical Ethical Decision-Making Literature," *Journal of Business Ethics* 117, no. 2 (2013): 221–59.

14. Virginia K. Bratton, "Affective Morality: The Role of Emotions in the Ethical Decision-Making Process" (doctoral diss., Florida State University, 2004), 12.

15. Rest and Narváez, *Moral Development in the Professions*, 233; Rest, *Moral Development*, 224.

16. Reuters, "Wife Says She and Madoff Tried Suicide," October 26, 2011, http://www.nytimes.com/2011/10/27/business/wife-says-she-and-madoff-tried-suicide.html?_r=1.

17. Tom Hays, Larry Neumeister, and Shlomo Shamir, "Extent of Madoff Fraud Now Estimated at Far below $50b," March 6, 2009, http://www.haaretz.com/news/extent-of-madoff-fraud-now-estimated-at-far-below-50b-1.271672.

18. Rest, *Moral Development*, 224.

19. Antonio Argandona, "The Stakeholder Theory and the Common Good," *Journal of Business Ethics* 17, no. 9 /10 (1998): 1095, http://www.jstor.org/stable/25073938.

20. James E. Post, Anne T. Lawrence, and James Weber, *Business and Society: Corporate Strategy, Public Policy, Ethics* (New York: McGraw-Hill Higher Education, 2002), 8.

21. Ibid., 8–9.

22. Ibid.

23. Ibid., 11.

24. Ibid., 12.

25. Ibid.

26. Ibid., 9.

27. Bart Victor and John B. Cullen, "The Organizational Bases of Ethical Work Climate," *Administrative Science Quarterly* 33, no. 1 (1988): 109, http://www.jstor.org/stable/2392857.

28. Ibid.

29. Raymond Baumhart, "How Ethical Are Businessmen?," *Harvard Business Review* 39 (1961): 6–19; Scott K. Jones and Kenneth M. Hiltebeitel, "Organizational Influence in a Model of the Moral Decision Process of Accountants," *Journal of Business Ethics* 14, no. 6 (1995): 417–31, http://www.jstor.org/stable/25072662; Geoffrey Soutar, Margaret M. McNeil, and Caron Molster, "The Impact of the Work Environment on Ethical Decision Making: Some Australian Evidence," *Journal of Business Ethics* 13, no. 5 (1994): 327–39, http://www.jstor.org/stable/25072537; William Verbeke, Cok Ouwerkerk, and Ed Peelen, "Exploring the Contextual and Individual Factors on Ethical Decision Making of Salespeople," *Journal of Business Ethics* 15, no. 11 (1996):1175–87, http://www.jstor.org/stable/25072842; Gary R. Weaver and Bradley R. Agle, "Religiosity and Ethical Behavior in Organizations: A Symbolic Interactionist Perspective," *Academy of Management Review* 27, no. 1 (2002): 77–97, http://www.jstor.org/stable/4134370.

30. Victor and Cullen, "The Organization Bases of Ethical Work Climate," 102.

31. Tim Barnett, "A Preliminary Investigation of the Relationship between Selected Organizational Characteristics and External Whistleblowing by Employees," *Journal of Business Ethics* 11, no. 12 (1992): 949–59, http://www.jstor.org/stable/25072360; Donald L. McCabe, Linda Klebe Trevino, and Kevin D. Butterfield, "The Influence of Collegiate and Corporate Codes of Conduct on Ethics-Related Behavior in the Workplace," *Business Ethics Quarterly* 6, no. 4 (1996): 461–76, http://www.jstor.org/stable/3857499; Linda Klebe Trevino and Stuart A. Youngblood, "Bad Apples in Bad Barrels: A Causal Analysis of Ethical Decision-Making Behavior," *Journal of Applied Psychology* 75, no. 4 (1990): 378–85.

32. Jeff Allen and Duane Davis, "Assessing Some Determinant Effects of Ethical Consulting Behavior: The Case of Personal and Professional Values," *Journal of Business Ethics* 12, no. 6 (1993): 449–58, http://www.jstor.org/stable/25072422; Gary R. Weaver, Linda Klebe Trevino, and Philip L. Cochran, "Corporate Ethics Practices in the Mid-1990's: An Empirical Study of the Fortune 1000," *Journal of Business Ethics* 18, no. 3 (1999): 283–94, doi:10.1023/A:1005726901050.

33. Charles R. Tittle and Alan R. Rowe, "Moral Appeal, Sanction Threat, and Deviance: An Experimental Test," *Social Problems* 20, no. 4 (1973): 488–98, http://www.jstor.org/stable/799710.

34. Tricia Bertram Gallant, "Twenty-First Century Forces Shaping Academic Integrity," *ASHE Higher Education Report* 33, no. 5 (2008): 56–78, http://onlinelibrary.wiley.com/doi/10.1002/aehe.3305/epdf.

35. Rebecca Volpe, Laura Davidson, and Matthew C. Bell, "Faculty Attitudes and Behaviors concerning Student Cheating," *College Student Journal* 42, no. 1 (2008): 165.

36. Claudio Lucifora and Marco Tonello, "Cheating and Social Interactions: Evidence from a Randomized Experiment in a National Evaluation Program," *Journal of Economic Behavior and Organization* 115 (July 2015): 45–66, doi:10.1016/j.jebo.2014.12.006.

37. R. Eric Reidenbach and Donald P. Robin, "Some Initial Steps toward Improving the Measurement of Ethical Evaluations of Marketing Activities," *Journal of Business Ethics* 7, no. 11 (1988): 871–79, http://www.jstor.org/stable/25071847; R. Eric Reidenbach and Donald P. Robin, "Toward the Development of a Multidimensional Scale for Improving Evaluations of Business Ethics," *Journal of Business Ethics* 9, no. 8 (1990): 639–53, http://www.jstor.org/stable/25072080.

38. Reidenbach and Robin, "Toward the Development of a Multidimensional Scale for Improving Evaluations of Business Ethics," 641.

39. Virginia K. Bratton and Connie Strittmatter, "To Cheat or Not to Cheat: The Role of Personality in Academic and Business Ethics," *Ethics and Behavior* 23, no. 6 (2013): 428, 434, http://www.tandfonline.com/doi/pdf/10.1080/10508422.2013.811077.

40. Bratton, "Affective Morality," 20–30; Bratton and Strittmatter, "To Cheat or Not to Cheat," 434.

41. Reidenbach and Robin, "Toward the Development of a Multidimensional Scale for Improving Evaluations of Business Ethics," 645.

42. Ibid., 646.

43. Ibid.

44. Ibid.

45. Ibid., 647.

46. Babson College, "New Approach to Business Ethics," http://www.babson.edu/Academics/teaching-research/gvv/Pages/new-approach-to-business-ethics-curriculum.aspx, accessed February 25, 2016.

47. Jane Mallor, A. James Barnes, L. Thomas Bowers, and Arlen Lanvardt, *Business Law: The Ethical, Global, and E-Commerce Environment* (Boston: McGraw-Hill, 2006); David P. Twomey, Marianne M. Jennings, and Stephanie M. Greene, *Anderson's Business Law and the Legal Environment, Comprehensive Volume* (Boston: Cengage Learning, 2016).

48. Joan C. Callahan, *Ethical Issues in Professional Life* (New York: Oxford University Press, 1988), 26.

49. Johannes Brinkmann, "Business and Marketing Ethics as Professional Ethics: Concepts, Approaches and Typologies," *Journal of Business Ethics* 41, no. 1–2 (2002): 159–77, http://www.jstor.org/stable/25074913.

50. Mark S. Frankel, "Professional Codes: Why, How, and with What Impact?," *Journal of Business Ethics* 8, no. 2–3 (1989): 111, http://www.jstor.org/stable/25071878.

51. Tim D. Bauer, "The Effects of Client Identity Strength and Professional Identity Salience on Auditor Judgments," *Accounting Review* 90, no. 1 (2015): 95–114, http://aaapubs.org/doi/abs/10.2308/accr-50863.

52. Jonathan Fuerbringer, "Buffett Sets Salomon Rules; Stock Up on Tisch's Buying," *New York Times*, August 27, 1991, http://www.nytimes.com/1991/08/27/business/buffett-sets-salomon-rules-stock-up-on-tisch-s-buying.html.

53. Janet Lowe, *Warren Buffet Speaks: Wit and Wisdom from the World's Greatest Investor* (New York: Wiley, 1998), 101–2.

54. Janet P. Near and Marcia P. Miceli, "Organizational Dissidence: The Case of Whistle-Blowing," *Journal of Business Ethics* 4, no. 1 (1985): 4, http://www.jstor.org/stable/25071466.

55. Michael J. Gundlach, Scott C. Douglas, and Mark J. Martinko, "The Decision to Blow the Whistle: A Social Information Processing Framework," *Academy of Management Review* 28 no. 1 (2003): 107–23, http://www.jstor.org/stable/30040692.

56. Janet P. Near and Marcia P. Miceli, "Effective Whistle-Blowing," *Academy of Management Review* 20, no. 3 (1995): 679–708, http://www.jstor.org/stable/258791.

57. Janet P. Near, Terry Morehead Dworkin, and Marcia P. Miceli, "Explaining the Whistle-Blowing Process: Suggestions from Power Theory and Justice Theory," *Organization Science* 4, no. 3 (1993): 393–411, http://www.jstor.org/stable/2634951.

58. Arthur P. Brief and Stephan J. Motowidlo, "Prosocial Organizational Behaviors," *Academy of Management Review* 11, no. 4 (1986): 710–25, http://www.jstor.org/stable/258391; Janet P. Near and Marcia P. Miceli, "Whistle-Blowing: Myth and Reality," *Journal of Management* 22 (1995): 507–27, doi:10.1177/014920639602200306.

59. Kohlberg, "Stage and Sequence," 347–480.

60. Richard T. Mowday, Richard M. Steers, and Lynne W. Porter, "The Measurement of Organizational Commitment," *Journal of Vocational Behavior* 14, no. 2 (1979): 224–47, http://www.sciencedirect.com/science/article/pii/0001879179900721.

61. Gundlach, Douglas, and Martinko, "The Decision to Blow the Whistle," 109.

62. Mary C. Gentile, *Giving Voice to Values: How to Speak Your Mind When You Know What's Right* (New Haven, CT: Yale University Press, 2010).

63. Babson College, "New Approach to Business Ethics," para. 2.

64. Rest, *Moral Development*, 224.

65. Mary C. Gentile, "Keeping Your Colleagues Honest," *Harvard Business Review* 88, no. 2 (2010): 114–15.

66. Ibid.

II

INTRODUCING PLAGIARISM AND ETHICS AWARENESS TRAINING

Part I provided an overview of academic integrity in the twenty-first century, an overview of plagiarism prevention instruction, and a justification for a new model: Plagiarism and Ethics Awareness Training (PEAT). We also provided a "crash course" in ethics for those not well versed in the subject area. Part II focuses on instructional techniques for incorporating PEAT into the curriculum. PEAT complements the pragmatic approach to plagiarism instruction, which addresses the mechanics of plagiarism prevention. We want to stress that PEAT is not meant to replace traditional instruction that teaches students how to cite sources, paraphrase, and attribute correctly. Rather, our position is that PEAT should be combined with traditional plagiarism prevention instruction to provide a holistic instructional approach—an approach that not only teaches students how to cite sources properly but also educates students that plagiarism is an ethical issue.

The information presented in part II addresses the design and implementation of a PEAT session. Chapter 4 explores pedagogical strategies that can be employed to create effective instruction sessions. This chapter draws from organizational behavior training and business ethics literature. We discuss transmissive and transformative approaches to teaching and how they are incorporated into PEAT. Expected outcomes of a PEAT session include students' abilities to acknowledge stakeholders, recognizing the university's moral expectations of them and strategies for addressing unethical actions when they occur. To achieve these outcomes, we focus on three pedagogical approaches: ethics instruction, case-based discussion, and role playing. By the end of chapter 4, readers will have an understanding of the pedagogical strategies recommended for designing a PEAT session.

Building off the pedagogical concepts introduced in chapter 4, chapter 5 describes the practical tools for teaching a PEAT session. We discuss five ethics-based models and provide key teaching elements for each. These models were created to serve a broad audience and can be used in conjunction with one another or independently. The decision to use one is based on the objectives for the session and the audience. The first three models—stakeholder analysis, theoretical criteria, and practical criteria—increase students' awareness of plagiarism as an ethical issue. These models also ask students to analyze scenarios to determine why it is an ethical issue. The final two models—changing the culture of plagiarism and giving voice to values—ask students how they would act when aware that an ethical violation has occurred. This model challenges students to think about whether they have a responsibility to report plagiarism if they believe that it is unethical and they know that it is a violation of the university's academic conduct code After introducing the five models, we provide sample curricula for a 50-minute one-shot instruction session (intracurricular), three 50-minute sessions that are an embedded module in a course (intercurricular), and a 50-minute session for an international student orientation (extracurricular).

The models introduced in chapter 5 can be used in any instructional setting. However, there are a variety of factors that an instructor faces when entering a classroom. Some factors are known in advance, such as class size, course level, technology available, and whether the professor will be present. Other factors, such as class makeup (traditional vs. nontraditional students) and class dynamics (engaged vs. nonengaged learners), will require the instructor to be able to adapt to the environment on the fly. Each of these factors provides unique challenges and opportunities. Chapter 6 focuses on implementing instruction and provides strategies and techniques for facilitating discussions and role-play activities in a small to medium-size class (fewer than 50 students), a high-enrollment class (more than 50 students), and an online environment.

3

Getting Started

Choosing Your Teaching Strategies for Plagiarism and Ethics Awareness Training

This chapter reviews a variety of pedagogical strategies that can be used when designing a Plagiarism and Ethics Awareness Training (PEAT) session. To establish core components that should be included during the instructional design phase, we focus on strategies employed when teaching business ethics and organizational behavior training. Not surprisingly, the processes and concepts that we review in this chapter overlap with common approaches used to teach information literacy skills.

Broadly speaking, there are two main philosophies for teaching. The transmissive approach involves the instructor passing knowledge onto students—commonly known as the sage on the stage. Students passively receive information from those who are experts in the field. Variations of this model include the incorporation of practice and feedback.[1] While the lecture is important to learning, engagement is a fundamental process to achieve a deep understanding of the material. In a transmissive approach, the onus to engage with the content is on students.

Sutherland-Smith provides the following insight into how transmissive teaching can be applied to plagiarism instruction.[2] First, information is conveyed to students through presentation and handouts that aim to increase students' awareness of what constitutes plagiarism and steps to avoid it. The class session consists primarily of a lecture and involves little discussion about the fuzzier aspects of plagiarism that may challenge students. Then tutorials are used to reinforce information introduced during the presentation. After the information is delivered, the onus is on the students to digest and apply the information. The underlining premise to Sutherland-Smith's explanation of transmissive plagiarism instruction is that once students understand the concept of plagiarism and its associated penalties, they avoid it.[3]

The transmissive model of teaching has value because many students come to a university with a cursory understanding of plagiarism, and they may not know the university penalties for plagiarism infringement. Further, a transmissive approach is typically used to introduce key ethical concepts to students. For these purposes, the transmissive approach is useful in the PEAT program. However, for students to retain and apply this information in a meaningful manner, a combination of trans-missive and transformational teaching is a more effective approach.

Transformative teaching expands on transmissive teaching because it creates an environment where students are challenged and expected to think critically about the topic at hand. Rather than having the instructor serve as the sole speaker, which is the common practice in transmissive teaching, a conversation takes place in the classroom. In this model, the instructor serves as a facilitator for classroom discussion. The peer-to-peer interaction among students and support from the instructor is how learning occurs. For this model to be successful, student engagement is crucial. Slavich and Zimbardo categorized elements of transformational teaching into five categories:

- Active learning
- Student-centered learning
- Collaborative learning
- Experiential learning
- Problem-based learning[4]

Transformational teaching lends itself nicely to PEAT which helps students recog-nize and analyze ethical implications of plagiarism and provides them with tools to voice their views when faced with an ethical dilemma. Through role-playing (active and experiential learning) and case-based discussion (active and collaborative learn-ing), students engage in the material and critically evaluate content to determine whether an act of plagiarism is unethical. The remainder of this chapter will focus on transformative pedagogical strategies that can be employed during a PEAT session. Business ethics pedagogy incorporates many transformative traits which we will use as the underlining basis for the pedagogical model we use. Specifically, we will focus on three learning outcomes and three instructional elements:

1. Outcomes: To increase the ethical awareness and sensitivity to plagiarism re-lated issues by doing the following:
   a. Acknowledging stakeholders
   b. Establishing the university's moral expectations of students
   c. Addressing unethical actions when they occur
2. Elements to incorporate into instruction to achieve outcomes:
   a. Ethics instruction
   b. Case-based discussion
   c. Role playing

This chapter provides the rationale for the building blocks to create an effective ethics-based plagiarism instruction session. Chapter 4 builds on the content presented in this chapter and provides sample exercises that can be incorporated into a PEAT session.

OUTCOMES FROM ETHICS-BASED INSTRUCTION

Bowden and Smythe[5] and Weber[6] have documented several strategies and techniques for ethics-based instruction. While their focus is on teaching ethics in the business schools and the corporate world, we have built off of these works to implement four of their concepts that can be incorporated into a PEAT program for use in any discipline.

Establishing realistic expectations and outcomes is important when designing PEAT. The overarching outcome for an instruction session is to increase the ethical awareness and sensitivity to plagiarism-related issues. In a 50-minute instruction session (or even, if fortunate enough, in multiple sessions dedicated to the topic), it is unlikely that you will modify students' ethical behaviors. In fact, there is minimal evidence to suggest that an ethics course can lead to students behaving more ethically.[7] However, these instruction sessions should serve as a catalyst to help increase a student's ethical sensitivity to issues related to academic integrity. This catalytic effect can be activated by having students work through plagiarism scenarios to determine whether the action taken by an individual in the scenario was ethical.[8] Through classroom discussions, students will reflect on their ethical stances on plagiarism, and this may provide clarity on how they might resolve potential ethical issues they may face.

ACKNOWLEDGING STAKEHOLDERS

Moral development occurs in several stages. In its most basic stage, individuals will evaluate the impact that an action will have on them and make a moral determination from that sole perspective. As moral development advances, individuals will begin to focus on the impact that an action has not only on themselves but also on others.[9] Given that the outcome of an instruction session is to heighten a student's ethical sensitivity, an integral component to achieving this is to have students conduct a stakeholder analysis.[10]

Stakeholders are internal or external individuals or groups impacted, either directly or indirectly, by an action. If you present students with a scenario in which a classmate takes a document from a report bank for a company in which he or she is interning and submits it for a class assignment, the discussion can begin by asking them who is potentially affected by the action. Students will generate a variety of responses ranging from the author of the work to fellow classmates to the professor. The goal of a stakeholder analysis is to have students understand that an act of plagiarism affects multiple groups. Students who understand and consistently apply this concept have fundamentally advanced from a selfish stage of moral development to one where they consider societal expectations and have started to internalize their moral principles.

ESTABLISHING THE UNIVERSITY'S MORAL EXPECTATIONS OF STUDENTS

Research suggests that the decision-making processes of individuals rely not only on their personal moral positions but also on their understandings of their organization's values.[11] Before making a decision with ethical consequences, individuals will likely compare their stance to ensure that it is consistent with the moral values of the institution. To facilitate this reconciliation of personal and organizational values, training sessions should incorporate documented elements of an organization's values, such as a code of ethics.[12] Ensuring that individuals are aware of their organization's moral compass will help them expand their behavior beyond an internal individual focus and align this behavior with organizational values.

To put this into context for an academic setting, an instruction session might include a transmissive presentation of the student code of conduct, which outlines acceptable academic behavior for students. Presenting this information informs students of the university's expectations of them. This ensures that all students, regardless of their backgrounds and prior education, are on the same page when it comes to understanding academic integrity at their university.

Conduct codes help identify and clarify what constitutes a breach of ethics and provide guidelines for possible responses. During the PEAT session, you may want to expand your discussion to encompass not only those behaviors that are unacceptable in the student code of conduct but also the implications of not reporting unethical acts. When a student is aware of an ethical violation and knows that it violates the code of conduct, he or she has an ethical duty to report the act.

DISCLOSING AN UNETHICAL ACTION

More often than not, individuals recognize when an unethical action occurs. However, individuals are often reluctant to report these actions because they feel that reporting the incident will not result in a change of behavior or policy, or they fear retribution from instructors and classmates if they do report the act. In chapter 2, we discussed whistle-blowing research and what influences an individual's decision to report wrongdoing. In general, individuals want to work in an environment that aligns with their personal ethics.[13] To create a culture that discourages wrongdoing, organizations must remove obstacles for individuals to report wrongdoing. Individuals need to feel that they will be protected from retaliation and that their reporting will effect positive change within the organization.

Creating a culture that discourages wrongdoing requires commitment by administrators to seriously address voiced concerns and protect those who bring forth their concerns about unethical behavior. However, individuals also need to develop the confidence to voice their concerns. Bowden and Smythe address this issue by incorporating a model in their ethics courses on developing "personal capabilities."[14] They believe that an ethics course should help students develop effective ways to communicate their ethical beliefs or concerns to others. In a safe classroom environment, students can learn how to advocate and voice their concerns. Developing that confidence to speak out when an unethical action occurs contributes to maintaining an ethical culture within an organization. When applying this principle to an academic setting, fear of retribution is minimal at the administrative levels. Most faculty, deans, and upper-level administrators are receptive to students who report ethical violations of the honor code. However, students are reluctant to report such violations for fear of the stigma associated with reporting the wrongdoing (i.e., "snitching"). Part of this fear can be minimized by helping students learn how to voice their concerns about violations of academic integrity in a way that reduces the emphasis on snitching and focuses on the importance of maintaining high ethical standards within the university.

ELEMENTS TO INCORPORATE INTO INSTRUCTION

The primary outcome of PEAT is to heighten students' ethical sensitivity to academic integrity violations by helping them consider more broadly who is affected by the action, conveying the university's position on academic misconduct, and helping students increase their comfort in recognizing and reporting ethical violations. In this section, we discuss strategies and exercises that can be incorporated into the instruction session to help achieve these outcomes.

Ethics Instruction

Incorporating ethics into a classroom instruction session is likely a new concept for librarians whose focus has been primarily on information literacy topics, such as research question design, searching strategies, and evaluating information. However, ethics instruction plays an important role in priming the *ethical sensitivity* of students, which is the central learning outcome in the PEAT program. Charting into this new territory may be unnerving for some. Research suggests that only a cursory amount of ethics theory instruction is needed because competing moral philosophies that underlie ethics theories often contradict one another (e.g., cultural relativism, right and wrong based on a set of cultural values, versus deontology, right and wrong based on an adherence to established rules). These contradictions can confuse students.[15] In addition, given that you have a limited amount of time with students, you do not want to get bogged down in ethical theory and not get to the core of the class content: students analyzing cases to make ethical determinations or practicing voicing their views on an action. Introduce ethics theory in a manner that is simple and easy to understand.

In the PEAT program, we use the Multidimensional Ethics Scale created by Robin and Reidenbach, which incorporates three broad ethical theories, to streamline our discussion of ethics theory. As discussed in chapter 2, this is an eight-question scale that evaluates sensitivity to moral intensity, cultural relativism, and contractualism. In our sessions we ask three basic questions: Is the action fair (moral intensity)? Is the action culturally acceptable (cultural relativism)? Does the action violate an un-written contract (contractualism)? These questions encompass key elements of each ethical theory but are presented in an understandable way to students.[16]

Problem-Based Discussion

A useful tool to help students recognize when an unethical act occurs is small-group discussions using problem-based case studies.[17] Problem-based discussion ad-dresses PEAT's central learning outcome, *heightening ethical sensitivity*, as well as its secondary outcomes, *acknowledging stakeholders* and *establishing the university's moral expectations of students*. Rossett and Emerson found that instructors use primarily case studies to enhance problem-solving and decision-making skills and to generate discussion and develop students' judgment in identified areas.[18] A case study can engage students in thought-provoking learning that may modify their attitudes.[19]

When using scenarios, it is important to ensure that they are realistic and relevant to students. If students perceive a scenario to be far-fetched or unlikely, they will not be challenged to critically think and reflect on the presented issue. Using real-life or high-profile examples of plagiarism can spark interest and allow for a more meaningful exchange of ideas and analysis.[20] In chapter 4, one model we discuss presents students with a plagiarism scenario that asks them to analyze the scenario using ethical theories and stakeholder analysis and assessing the university's position. Using those tools, students make a determination about whether the presented act was unethical. By having them analyze a problem-based scenario through an ethical lens, we expect that students will be able to view plagiarism violations in a new light.

As the instructor, you facilitate the discussion by synthesizing information pre-sented by students, clarifying student comments, and expanding on points that were raised.[21] Through this process, an active learning environment is created in which the students explore the scenario from various viewpoints. Students are likely to be at different levels of moral development. One student may determine the ethicality of a scenario based on how he or she is impacted, while another student may evaluate the ethicality of the action based on the impact it may have on individuals.[22] View these variations in moral development not as a challenge but as an opportunity. You can guide the group discussion to highlight different viewpoints and encourage students to reflect on their peers' comments. As students evaluate the scenario from a variety of perspectives, they may begin to heighten their ethical sensitivity to plagiarism-related issues.

Role Playing

One of the objectives that Bowden and Smythe outlined for an effective ethics course is "build personal capabilities,"[23] which is the ability for an individual to effectively communicate his or her moral stance to others. As with most things, the way one gains proficiency is through practice. Role playing offers an opportunity for students to practice within a safe and low-stakes environment. This method addresses PEAT's central learning outcome, *heightening ethical sensitivity*, as well as a secondary learning outcome, *addressing unethical behaviors*. When students recognize that an unethical action occurred, many feel compelled to address it but are unsure about the best way to approach the discussion. To whom should they communicate their concern? How do they initiate the conversation?

Role playing can help students develop the skills to effectively communicate their ethical stance on an issue. Role playing invokes critical thinking, moral deliberation, and emotion. There are several benefits associated with role-playing activities.[24] First, role playing provides a safe and experimental environment for students. When role-playing a scenario, students are able to try out a variety of responses to see which is most compelling. Because students are not under scrutiny (the character is), they may feel liberated to share or discuss issues they not do otherwise. Second, role playing simulates reality.[25] Students are presented a realistic scenario and role-play how they would respond to the situation.[26] By practicing their responses, students develop proficiency for and comfort with how they can ethically address a plagiarism situation. Finally, role playing can be an enjoyable activity. Students receive feedback from their peers and instructor on the effectiveness of their role play. Having students actively engaged in an activity increases students' enthusiasm and provides incentives for them to embrace the concepts introduced.[27]

While there are many options for role playing, we recommend using the Giving Voice to Values (GVV) model developed by Mary C. Gentile.[28] Students are presented with a scenario in which they are aware that an unethical action has occurred and are asked to develop a script to address the situation. What we like about this model is that the presented scenario has already determined an action to be unethical; the emphasis of the role play is how students will take action to voice their concerns. Because many students are reluctant to report an honor code violation, having the decision to report made for them can be empowering because it removes the stigma of being considered a snitch. GVV is effective because the model is based on several assumptions, including the following three that we believe are most prevalent:

1. Students want to voice their values: Inherently, students recognize an unethical action and want to address it but have concerns about doing so.

2. Students are more likely to voice their values if they have practiced how to respond to potential counterarguments: If students can anticipate and address the rationalizations made by the person they are confronting, then they will be better able to navigate the conversation.
3. If students believe it is possible to prepare and act on their values, they will be more likely to do so: If students feel confident that they can deliver a compelling message, they will be more likely to speak out. Students also have to be confident in their ability to handle any politics that may arise from their discussions.[29]

In a safe classroom environment, students can practice how they would address the issue of academic dishonesty. They can anticipate how an individual may rationalize his or her actions and explain how those rationalizations are not viable arguments. Critically analyzing one's viewpoints, drafting scripts, and putting the script into action by verbally presenting the case creates "muscle memory," which can help those who lack confidence speak out against an unethical action.[30]

While GVV comes from the perspective that individuals want to voice their values, this type of role playing can also be beneficial to those who do not necessarily believe that an ethical violation occurred and do not feel that it needs to be reported. Because the scenario is set and a script is needed to address the issues, the students have the opportunity to examine their own beliefs about the scenario in addition to viewing the issues from a perspective other than their own.[31]

PEAT uses a combination of transmissive and transformational teaching strategies. Transmissive modes can be used to provide an introduction to ethics theory, but the majority of the PEAT session will utilize transformative teaching methods, such as case-based problems discussed in small groups and role playing. By engaging students and making them active participants in the classroom, instructors are more likely to achieve the overarching goal of heightening students' ethical sensitivity to plagiarism-related issues. This chapter served to introduce the models that can be used in the classroom. Chapter 4 provides in-depth examples of exercises that an instructor can use to design his or her own instruction session.

NOTES

1. David H. Jonassen and Susan M. Land, *Theoretical Foundations of Learning Environments* (Mahwah, NJ: Lawrence Erlbaum Associates, 2000), iv.
2. Wendy Sutherland-Smith, *Plagiarism, the Internet and Student Learning* (New York: Routledge, 1998), 137.
3. Ibid., 135–46.
4. George M. Slavich and Philip G. Zimbardo, "Transformational Teaching: Theoretical Underpinnings, Basic Principles, and Core Methods," *Educational Psychology Review* 24, no. 4 (2012): 572–73, http://link.springer.com/article/10.1007/s10648-012-9199-6/fulltext.html.

5. Peter Bowden and Vanya Smythe, "Theories on Teaching & Training in Ethics," *EJBO—Electronic Journal of Business Ethics and Organization Studies* 13, no. 2 (2008): 20, http://ejbo.jyu.fi/pdf/ejbo_vol13_no2_pages_19-26.pdf.

6. John A. Weber, "Business Ethics Training: Insights from Learning Theory," *Journal of Business Ethics* 70, no. 1 (2007): 61–85, http://link.springer.com/article/10.1007%2Fs10551-006-9083-8.

7. Bowden and Smythe, "Theories on Teaching & Training in Ethics," 20.

8. Ibid.

9. Weber, "Business Ethics Training," 62.

10. Ibid., 64.

11. Ibid., 63.

12. Ibid., 63; Bowden and Smythe, "Theories on Teaching & Training in Ethics," 20.

13. Bowden and Smythe, "Theories on Teaching & Training in Ethics," 21.

14. Ibid., 22.

15. Ibid., 24.

16. R. Eric Reidenbach and Donald P. Robin, "Toward the Development of a Multidimensional Scale for Improving Evaluations of Business Ethics," *Journal of Business Ethics* 9, no. 8 (1990): 639–53, http://www.jstor.org/stable/25072080.

17. Weber, "Business Ethics Training," 63; Bowden and Smythe, "Theories on Teaching & Training in Ethics," 23.

18. Jay Alden and Judith Kirkhorn, "Case Studies," in *The ASTD Training and Development Handbook*, ed. Robert L. Craig (New York: McGraw-Hill, 1996), 504.

19. Ibid., 500.

20. Cara Bradley, *Plagiarism Education and Prevention: A Subject-Driven Case-Based Approach* (Oxford: Chandos, 2011), 11.

21. Ibid., 506.

22. Weber, "Business Ethics Training," 64.

23. Bowden and Smythe, "Theories on Teaching & Training in Ethics," 24.

24. Morry van Ments, *The Effective Use of Role-Play: Practical Techniques for Improving Learning* (London: Kogan Page, 1999), 13.

25. Ibid., 14.

26. Suchismita Bhattacharjee, "Effectiveness of Role-Playing as a Pedagogical Approach to Construction Education," *50th ASC Annual International Conference Proceedings* 2014: 1, http://ascpro0.ascweb.org/archives/cd/2014/paper/CERT199002014.pdf.

27. van Ments, *The Effective Use of Role-Play*, 15.

28. Mary C. Gentile. *Giving Voice to Values: How to Speak Your Mind When You Know What's Right* (New Haven, CT: Yale University Press, 2010).

29. Ibid., 224–27.

30. Ibid., 7.

31. Olusegun Agboola Sogunro, "Efficacy of Role-Playing Pedagogy in Training Leaders: Some Reflections," *Journal of Management Development* 23, no. 4 (2004): 358, http://dx.doi.org/10.1108/02621710410529802.

4

Designing Your Content

The Curricular Building Blocks of Plagiarism and Ethics Awareness Training

In the previous chapter, pedagogical approaches for designing Plagiarism Awareness and Ethics Training (PEAT) sessions were introduced. Shorter sessions using a case-based approach that engage cognitively tend to be most effective. This chapter introduces five ethics-based instructional models that can be used independently or in combination with one another. Each model is defined and explained in depth throughout the chapter, but a summary of the models can be found in table 4.1:

1. Stakeholder analysis[1]
2. Ethical decision making using theoretical criteria[2]
3. Ethical decision making using practical criteria[3]
4. Student role in changing the culture of plagiarism[4]
5. Giving Voice to Values[5]

To demonstrate how these models can function in a PEAT session, we adapted the following scenario from Harris's examples in *The Plagiarism Handbook*[6] to illustrate similarities and differences between these instructional models:

Jane is taking a finance class and is assigned a 10- to 15-page paper that requires her to analyze the financial health of a company. The paper accounts for 35 percent of the final grade. Jane is currently interning at a local financial firm and has been quite busy with her internship and other class assignments. Her financial analysis assignment is due in two days. Knowing that she doesn't have time to write a paper, she takes a report from a "report bank" at the firm, makes slight modifications to it, and submits it to her professor.

Table 4.1. Instructional Models for PEAT

Model	Learning Objective	Teaching Approach	Questions Asked or Tasks Assigned to Students
Stakeholder analysis	1. To increase awareness that plagiarism is an ethical violation 2. To analyze why plagiarism is an ethical violation	• Case-based scenario • Small-group discussion • Debrief as class	• Who is affected by the action?
Theoretical criteria	1. To increase awareness that plagiarism is an ethical violation 2. To analyze why plagiarism is an ethical violation	• Case-based scenario • Small-group discussion • Debrief as class	• Was the action fair? (moral equity) • Is the action culturally acceptable? (relativism) • Does the action violate an unwritten contract? (contractualism)
Practical criteria	1. To increase awareness that plagiarism is an ethical violation 2. To analyze why plagiarism is an ethical violation	• Case-based scenario • Small-group discussion • Debrief as class	• Does the action fall within usual standards? • If I were [name], would I be willing to see this action on the front page of a newspaper? • Do you believe [name] friends and loved ones would approve?
Changing the culture	1. To analyze why plagiarism is an ethical violation 2. To increase student awareness of their responsibility to report an act of plagiarism if they believe the action is unethical and violates university policy	• Case-based scenario • Small-group discussion • Debrief as class	• What do you do? (discuss the options available to you and be prepared to select one and justify your selection)
Giving Voice to Values	1. To provide tools that allow students to voice their concerns about an unethical action that occurred	• Script-writing workshop • Presentation of script • Peer and instructor feedback	• Script writing and presenting

STAKEHOLDER ANALYSIS

A stakeholder analysis[7] examines, "those groups and individuals who can affect or be affected" by an action. Typically, stakeholder theory has been used to discuss the impacts of an action in business situations, but it can be applied to academic integrity, including plagiarism and cheating, as well. This model also incorporates stakeholder theory and aspects of utilitarianism. In its most basic definition, utilitarianism focuses on the impact that an act has on the collective rather than the individual good.[8] The majority of today's college students are part of the Millennial generation, and studies have shown that they tend to be more individualistic and self-focused than other generations.[9] Asking students to think more broadly about the impact of an action on a society may help broaden their thinking about plagiarism as an ethical issue.

To break this down for students who do not have a background in ethics theory and who may not fully understand the nomenclature associated with utilitarianism and stakeholder theory, have students read Jane's scenario and in small groups answer the following question:

- Who is affected by Jane's actions?

This question, although simple in nature, asks students to take a utilitarian approach and apply stakeholder theory to the scenario. This question requires students to identify the stakeholders involved in Jane's actions. Unethical acts rarely impact only the person performing them; many others are impacted even if only tangentially. Sadler identified 10 arguments as to why plagiarism is unethical. Many of the arguments are based on the impacts the action has on an individual or group.[10]

In the presented scenario, the following groups or individuals are potentially affected by the action that Jane has taken:

1. The author of the report: When Jane took the report, she was stealing the intellectual property of the report's author. While the author may never find out that the ideas presented in the report were stolen and would likely suffer no copyright infringement, as the paper submitted would not be published, a theft of ideas did nevertheless occur.[11]
2. The professor teaching the course: Professors work on the assumption that the papers they grade are the genuine ideas and efforts of their students. Professors grade papers to provide feedback to help enhance a student's knowledge. When Jane turned in a paper that was not her own, she was in essence deceiving her professor.[12]
3. Jane: Jane herself is affected. By not submitting her own work, she is not acting in the spirit that one ought to have when attending a university. Students go to a university to be educated. Jane is denying herself this opportunity. She is also enabling several habits that will not benefit her in the future, such as laziness

and dishonesty.[13] Behavior practiced in an academic setting tends to translate to the workplace. Studies show that there is a positive relationship between unethical behavior in university and workplace settings.[14]

4. Classmates taking the course: Jane's classmates are potentially affected by her actions. By submitting a trained analyst's report, she is unfairly setting a higher bar for her classmates. This is especially true if the papers are graded on a curve.[15] (This scenario can be taken even further to include students not in the class but in the academic department. If Jane submitted a paper that was not her own and the professor did not catch it, then she could get an A in the class given that the paper was 35 percent of the final grade. Jane may not know much about financial analysis, but given that she got an A in the class and had an internship, she could be very attractive to recruiters. If hired by a firm, her employer would quickly learn that she does not have the knowledge they were led to believe. If a firm has a bad experience, it could decide not to recruit at the institution in the future. This could affect other students' opportunities to obtain a job at a reputable firm. This scenario can especially hold true at institutions that are geographically isolated where recruiting visits are a destination and not a stop at one university in a city of many.)

5. The university: Jane's actions can also affect the university. Similarly to the ways in which a student is potentially affected by Jane's actions, the degree offered by the university can become devalued, thus affecting its reputation. In addition, in a time when student tuition and loan costs are skyrocketing and society is questioning the value of a college degree, any negativity associated with a university can have an adverse reputational impact.[16]

6. Future employers: Potential employers can also be impacted by Jane's actions. If she has a pattern of plagiarizing throughout her academic career, she will not likely have the skills that are needed to be an effective employee when she enters the workforce. An organization that hires her either will likely have to invest heavily in training to get her to an acceptable level of performance or may decide after a period of time that she is untrainable and terminate her. In either case, the organization suffers from Jane's actions.

ETHICAL DECISION MAKING USING THEORETICAL CRITERIA

Using some of the ethical theories introduced in chapter 2, students can apply theoretical criteria to Jane's scenario to dissect their decision about the ethicality of the action. Recognizing that students are not likely to be well versed in ethical theory, we suggest using questions from the Multidimensional Ethics Scale (MES) developed by Reidenbach and Robin.[17] As discussed in chapter 2, this scale consists of eight questions that ask users to rate their perceptions of an action that is presented in an ethical scenario. The MES was initially created to measure perceptions of ethical behavior in business.[18] More recently, its application has expanded to include measurements of ethical perceptions on academic integrity issues.[19] In chapter 6, we revisit the MES as an assessment tool to evaluate the effectiveness of PEAT.

For instructional purposes, three of the eight questions are used. Similarly to stakeholder analysis, the questions may seem simple. However, each one is rooted in ethical theory. This model pairs well with stakeholder analysis because each question can be applied to the various stakeholders:

- Is the action fair?
- Is the action culturally acceptable?
- Does the action violate an unwritten contract?

Is the Action Fair? (Moral Equity Theory)

The core of moral equity theory is justice and fairness. These are values that may have been instilled in users at a young age.[20] Asking students to answer this question in relation to the stakeholders identified allows them to practice ethical decision making. Through discussion, students should come to the realization that Jane's action potentially results in a higher reward for less effort, particularly compared with her classmates. This imbalance of effort and reward between Jane and other stakeholders results in an unfair situation.

Is the Action Culturally Acceptable? (Cultural Relativism)

Rooted in relativism, this question delves into societal views of an action. The acceptability of an action when viewed through a relativistic lens may vary, depending on the values and beliefs of the relevant social groups.[21] In this exercise, each stakeholder is a referent group. When discussing whether Jane's action is ethical in the context of relativism, students typically recognize that submitting a paper that is not an original work by the student is not culturally acceptable among the university, professor, and author stakeholder groups. They may challenge whether plagiarism deviates from the norms of classmates as a stakeholder group. Students may believe that it is culturally acceptable to plagiarize; for example, this acceptance of plagiarism may have fueled the creation of paper banks within student organizations. If presented with this argument, instructors can guide the discussion by asking the students why it is culturally acceptable and how students can help change that perception. Some ways to influence this discussion can be to informally apply *practical criteria* (discussed below). For example, using the *front-page-of-the-newspaper test*, you can ask students to consider whether Jane would want that action to appear on the front page of the student newspaper for all of their peers to see.

Does the Action Violate an Unwritten Contract? (Contractualism)

Contractualism explores social contracts and whether there is either an explicit or an implicit understanding that exists as to what is considered ethical behavior.[22] For many professors and institutions, the student *social contract* is made explicit in the student handbook or code of conduct contract that students sign for a class, so the expectations are very clear from the beginning. However, it may elicit an interesting discussion to query students about whether there is an unwritten understanding among them that each will behave ethically during the course of the semester. When students come together as classmates at the start of the semester, does it go without saying that students agree that they will submit their own work? Or is each student out for him- or herself, all self-serving actions being on the table? It is likely that the answers to these questions will be consistent with how students answer the cultural relativism question: *Is it culturally acceptable among students to plagiarize and submit work that is not their own?* This further establishes and reinforces contextual norms for ethical responses to plagiarism in your academic environment.

ETHICAL DECISION MAKING USING PRACTICAL CRITERIA

Using a model that applies practical criteria to an ethical situation may resound more with students. We have found that replacing theoretical criteria with a series of questions representing practical criteria allows the students to grapple with a situation in a way that may be more familiar and comfortable to them.[23] Parts of this model may work well with international students whose native social groups may not find plagiarism to be an ethical violation. After presenting Jane's scenario, ask students the following questions, which represent practical criteria:

- Do Jane's actions fall within the usual standards?
- If you were Jane, would you be willing to see this action on the front page of a newspaper?
- Do you believe Jane's friends and loved ones would approve?

Do Jane's Actions Fall within the Usual Standards?

Students may ask what is meant by "usual standards." Typically, university policy and course syllabi establish the usual standards for students. Discuss the university's policy on academic misconduct and the types of behavior that construe misconduct. By attending classes at this university, students have consented to what makes up a contractual obligation to adhere to the university's academic and behavioral standards. Clearly defining this expectation helps international students understand that what is acceptable in their home culture may not be consistent with the expectations of the university.

In this instance, Jane's action does not fall within the acceptable standards of the university, as most student handbooks state that the submission of a paper that is not one's own is prohibited and punishable.

If You Were Jane, Would You Be Willing to See This Action on the Front Page of a Newspaper?

The front-page-of-the-newspaper test takes a global perspective by comparing an individual's action to the community's values and ethics. This question brings public recognition for an action to the forefront. How would one feel if an act one committed were the headline of a national newspaper? If one would be pleased to see one's actions in the headline news, then the action is more than likely acceptable (*Jane Smith, Fulbright Scholar!*). If one would be shamed by having an action highlighted in the paper, then it is likely not acceptable (*Jane Smith, Plagiarist!*). At the very least, this test requires students to pause before committing unethical acts in order to consider how they would justify these actions to a public audience.

Do You Believe Jane's Friends and Loved Ones Would Approve?

This question embodies constructs from moral equity theory. At the heart of moral equity theory is upbringing and the morals one is taught as a child from parents and family.[24] Is Jane acting within the moral framework of her upbringing?

This question differs from the newspaper headline question in that it focuses on how Jane thinks her intimate peer groups of family and friends would feel about her behavior. In contrast to the newspaper test, there isn't widespread publicity and public scrutiny about the action. This test is more personal because it asks students to place themselves in Jane's shoes and consider how those closest to her would feel about her behavior.

THE STUDENT'S ROLE IN CHANGING THE CULTURE OF PLAGIARISM

The three models presented above focus solely on the ethicality of Jane's submission of a paper that she did not write. Another approach takes the scenario in a different direction by switching the focus from Jane's action to what a bystander should do. Harris[25] introduced the concept of "You Be the Judge," in which students are privy to knowledge that a classmate plagiarized a paper. Having this knowledge, what should they do? To ascertain student responses to this type of scenario, we make subtle modifications to Jane's scenario:

> You and Jane are taking a finance class and are assigned a 10- to 15-page paper that requires you to analyze the financial health of a company. The paper accounts for 35

percent of the final grade. You and Jane are currently interning at a local financial firm and this has kept you both quite busy. The day after the assignment was due, you and Jane were lamenting about the assignment. You mentioned that the paper took you many hours to complete. Jane laughs and says that it didn't take her nearly that long because she took a report from a "report bank" at the firm, made some slight modifications, and submitted it to the professor.

Present students with the following questions:

- You know that Jane has submitted a paper for the assignment that is not her own work. What do you do? Discuss the options available to you and be prepared to select one and justify your selection.

Most students readily recognize that submitting someone else's work as their own is unethical, but when this question is added to the scenario, interesting discussions with students occur. There is a wide spectrum of actions available to the students, including the following:

- Saying nothing
- Confronting Jane about her actions
- Anonymously tipping off the professor to Jane's actions
- Visiting the professor to inform him about what Jane has done
- Discussing Jane's actions with the supervisor of the company for which they intern

Students usually identify all of these options, and the option they choose, more often than not, is to say nothing. Students know that Jane behaved unethically, but overwhelmingly they do not feel that they are responsible for holding Jane accountable for her actions. Students provide the following justifications for not saying or doing anything:

- It's none of their business what Jane does: Students take a very individualistic stance. Many students strongly adhere to the principle that each person is his or her own keeper and responsible for his or her own actions. It is not their place to confront Jane about actions they believe to be unethical.
- Jane's actions won't affect them: The theme of individualism plays into this rationale as well. Students do not believe that Jane's actions will affect them. If they just do their own work and focus on themselves, they believe they will be fine. You can challenge them on this principle by asking them if their view would change if the papers were graded on a curve. In addition, you could walk them through a scenario where Jane was hired by a company that visited the university's job fair. On hiring her and realizing that she was not knowledgeable in financial analyses, they decide to no longer recruit from the university, thus eliminating a potential job opportunity at that firm.

- No one wants to be a snitch: The stigma of being known as a snitch among peers outweighs any willingness to address an issue that they think is wrong. In essence, it is more acceptable to be a plagiarist than a snitch. For this to not hold true, there needs to be a cultural shift that leads to a decrease in the acceptability of plagiarism. Alternatively, there needs to be a shift where confronting another person and holding him or her accountable for his or her actions (i.e., snitching) does not make the confronter a pariah.
- The professor is responsible for recognizing that Jane's paper is not her own: It is important not to discount this argument. Professors are responsible for designing assignments that make it difficult for students to plagiarize. In addition, courses should have enough assessment opportunities that a professor would recognize that the paper submitted is not indicative of Jane's knowledge in financial analysis. Acknowledge that professors do have a responsibility and that students also have a responsibility to shape an ethical culture. Perhaps in this instance, Jane wrote quality assignments previously, so no red flags were raised for the professor. Students will also mention that plagiarism software (e.g., Turnitin) would catch that this paper belongs to another. In this scenario, the paper taken from a report bank at the firm is a nonpublic/nonpublished paper, so it would not be caught through plagiarism software such as Turnitin. Hence, in this modified Jane's scenario, the professor might not detect Jane's plagiarism unless another student reports it.

As the class discusses multiple rationales for not reporting Jane's actions, you can push students to consider whether they have a *responsibility* to report plagiarism if they believe that it is unethical and they know that it is a violation of the university's academic conduct code. In many instances, students' reluctance to confront Jane or inform her professor of the ethical violation can be attributed to the stigma associated with whistle-blowing. Whistle-blowing is most commonly associated with business, but conceptually many of the elements of whistle-blowing research can be applied to academic integrity issues. Hoffman and McNulty developed the Universal Dignity Theory of Whistleblowing, which defines criteria that make whistle-blowing not only permissible but also an ethical obligation. The following must exist for whistle-blowing to be ethical:

- "Compelling evidence of nontrivial illegal or unethical actions done by an organization or its employees that are deemed to violate the dignity of one or more of its stakeholders [and]
- . . . a lack of knowledge within the organization of the wrongdoing or failure by the organization to take corrective actions"[26]

The only caveat relieving an individual from compelled action is the plausible evidence that severe retaliation would occur for whistle-blowing.[27] However, this caveat may be moot if the consequences of not reporting an offense outweigh any retaliation from reporting the behavior.

These criteria can be applied to Jane's scenario to demonstrate that there is an ethical obligation to report acts of plagiarism when an individual has knowledge that they occurred. Jane told the student that she submitted a paper from the report bank at the firm, so there is evidence that an unethical action was done that harms stakeholders (professor, classmates, and firm). The professor does not know that Jane has submitted a paper that is not her own, so there is a lack of knowledge within the organization (university). The student has no credible evidence that by informing the professor of the action, he or she would be retaliated against.

An instructor can also challenge students to discuss what silence on the matter may mean. Is silence a tacit form of approval? Does inaction contribute to a culture of unethical behavior?

GIVING VOICE TO VALUES

Ethics training helps students recognize an ethical issue and apply an analysis to identify what is unethical about the behavior. Not only do we hope that ethics training helps students modify their perceptions about the ethicality of plagiarism, but we also hope that it enables them to voice their values when confronted with an unethical situation. If we can get students to a point where they feel that they should say something but do not know how to approach the conversation, the Giving Voice to Values (GVV) model[28] can be used to help them find their voice so they can effectively communicate their values.

The GVV model was introduced in chapter 2 and provides strategies that enable students to speak their values when confronted with an unethical situation. Whereas the first four models focus on awareness and analysis of situations, GVV, through a series of scripts and role playing, provides students with a tool for action. Students are presented with a scenario in which they are the protagonists who are aware that an act of cheating occurred. This model does not ask students to determine whether the action is unethical. That has already been determined. It has also been determined that the right thing to do is to address the issue. The question presented asks students *how* they take action. Once you determine the right response to an ethical dilemma, how do you *implement* that response? Students are asked to write a script that details the conversation they would have or the letter they would write addressing their thoughts on the action.

This model's goals are twofold. First, a student or group of students must craft a script that helps them address the ethical issue. In Jane's modified scenario, students need to decide with whom they will discuss the issue. After students prepare their scripts, they present them to the class for feedback and coaching. The presentation of the script is important. By verbally presenting their scripts, students get practice stating their concerns about a situation. The instructor and classmates can discuss what parts of the script were compelling and offer suggestions for improvement. The act of verbally articulating a concern can arm students with the confidence that they can voice their values in a meaningful way that can lead to a satisfaction that they did not stand idly by when witnessing or being privy to an unethical act. Active learning techniques, such as role playing and script rehearsal, engage students more than traditional forms of teaching because they are interacting with materials that require them to think critically about a situation. This engagement leads to an enhanced understanding of concepts presented.[29]

Each student's voice is unique, so the scripts will vary, but elements they may want to consider as they prepare their script include the following:

- To whom are they going to voice their concern? Will they be talking to Jane, the professor, the manager at the firm, or someone else?
- What is it that the students hope to achieve?
- How can students minimize any potential risks to their actions (being considered a snitch, etc.)?
- What arguments will they use to present their justification (lack of fairness or impact on others)?
- What counterarguments can they expect to hear (it doesn't affect them, everyone is doing it)?

PUTTING IT ALL TOGETHER

The models presented can be used independently or in combination with one another. Depending on the time allotted to an instruction session and the objectives and goals for the session, an instructor could dedicate an entire 50-minute session to ethics-based scenarios. If time is limited, an instructor could incorporate one or two of these models so that 15 to 20 minutes is spent discussing plagiarism as an ethical issue. Each model requires a plagiarism scenario to analyze. This book's appendix contains sample scenarios that can be used.

Below we present sample curriculums designed for a range of instructional settings:

1. Intracurricular approach 1: A 50-minute instruction session dedicated almost exclusively to PEAT
2. Intercurricular approach: A course-based module consisting of three 50-minute sessions on plagiarism prevention skills, PEAT, and voicing values
3. Extracurricular approach: A 50-minute session for a noncurricular event, such as international student orientation

Intracurricular Approach 1: A 50-Minute Instruction Session Dedicated Almost Exclusively to PEAT

In this instruction session, the first 10 to 15 minutes provides a review of why we should cite sources and types of information that needs to be cited. The remaining 35 to 40 minutes is focused on case-based ethics instruction.

Why We Cite Sources (5 Minutes)

- Goal: To demonstrate that there is value in citing sources and that it benefits several groups.
- Teaching strategy: Ask students why we cite sources when writing a paper. Allow the students to come up with the reasons. Fill in any reasons that they may miss.
- Main points to cover:
  o Strengthens the writer's arguments and increases credibility
  o Shows respect for the author's intellectual efforts and ideas
  o Assists the reader if they want to follow up on a point made in the paper[30]

When to Cite Sources (10 Minutes)

- Goal: Provide an overview of what types of sources should be cited and what does not need to be cited.
- Teaching strategy: Present slides with examples asking if they need to cite the source. Have students explain why or why not.
  o Example: You are writing a paper on the challenges that small business owners face in a declining economy. Your father owns a local business in town, and you interview him for the paper and include a quote from him. Do you need to cite your dad?
- Main points to cover:
  o Common knowledge (does not need to be cited)
  o Ideas (cite)
  o Government information (cite)
  o Interviews or email exchanges (cite)

PEAT (35 Minutes)

- Goal: To present plagiarism as an ethical issue.
- Teaching strategy: In this scenario, three of the five models are incorporated into the scenario. Present a scenario. Break the class into small groups of four to six students and have them review the scenario and answer the questions presented. Have each group present their findings to the class and finish with a class discussion. If time allows, an additional scenario can be presented and discussed.
- Example scenario:
  o You and Jane are taking a finance class and are assigned a 10- to 15-page paper that requires you to analyze the financial health of a company. The paper accounts for 35 percent of the final grade. You and Jane are currently interning at a local financial firm, and this has kept you both quite busy. The day after the assignment was due, you and Jane were lamenting about the assignment. You mentioned that the paper took you many hours to complete. Jane laughs and says that it didn't take her nearly that long because she took

a report from a "report bank" at the firm, made some slight modifications, and submitted it to the professor.

- Who are the stakeholders affected by Jane's action? (stakeholder analysis)
- Was the action fair? Was the action culturally acceptable? Does the action violate an unspoken promise? (applying ethical theories—explain to the students how each question applies to an ethical theory)
- You know that Jane has submitted a paper for the assignment that is not her own work. What do you do? Discuss the options available to you and be prepared to select one and justify your selection. (changing the culture of plagiarism)

Intercurricular Approach: A Course-Based Module Consisting of Three 50-Minute Sessions on Plagiarism Prevention Skills, PEAT, and Voicing Values

If able to have an information literacy component consisting of three classroom sessions embedded in a course, a library instructor has much more flexibility in designing an instruction session that incorporates PEAT. In this design, session 1 provides an overview of plagiarism and tips for avoiding it. This is a practical tools-based session. Session 2 introduces PEAT, in which students use a case-based approach to analyze why an action is considered unethical. The final session is a continuation of PEAT and incorporates the GVV model in which students develop and present scripts on how they would address an issue of plagiarism to a stakeholder. Each session builds off the previous session and provides comprehensive coverage of plagiarism from both preventive and ethical perspectives.

Session 1: Overview of Academic Integrity at the Institution and Proper Source Attribution

- Goal: This session provides a basic overview of what plagiarism is, how to attribute correctly, what does not need to be cited, and suggestions for note taking.
- Teaching strategy: This is a presentation-based session, but the instructor can add elements to increase participation by providing examples and asking students if the information presented is considered plagiarism and, if so, how can it be corrected.
- Main points to cover:
  o Why we cite sources (strengthens the writer's arguments and increases credibility, shows respect for another's intellectual property, assists the reader if he or she wants to follow up on a point made in the paper)
  o Define plagiarism (dictionary definition and definition in the university's student code of conduct)
  o Examples of plagiarism and how it can be modified to be acceptable:
    - Submitting another's paper as his or her own
    - Copying text verbatim and omitting quotation marks and sources

- ■ Paraphrasing and not citing sources
- ■ Recycling papers (why it isn't acceptable and reference university policy)
- o What you do not need to cite (common knowledge and own ideas)
- o Note-taking strategies (dual column note taking and index cards)
- o Tips to avoid plagiarizing
- o Introduction to citation styles used in discipline (if time allows)

Session 2: Introducing PEAT

This session is very similar to the intracurricular instruction presented above. The main difference is that the entire class can be focused on introducing ethics into plagiarism training since much of the preliminary content introduced in the intra-curricular session was covered in session 1 of the intercurricular instruction sessions.

- • Goal: To present plagiarism as an ethical issue.
- • Teaching strategy: Instructors should be able to cover two or three scenarios during the class period. Present a scenario. Break the class into small groups of four to six students and have them review the scenario and answer the questions presented. Have each group present their findings to the class and finish with a class discussion.
- • Scenario 1:
  - o You and Jane are taking a finance class and are assigned a 10- to 15-page paper that requires you to analyze the financial health of a company. The paper accounts for 35 percent of the final grade. You and Jane are currently interning at a local financial firm, and this has kept you both quite busy. The day after the assignment was due, you and Jane were lamenting about the as-signment. You mentioned that the paper took you many hours to complete. Jane laughs and says that it didn't take her nearly that long because she took a report from a "report bank" at the firm, made some slight modifications, and submitted it to the professor.
    - ■ Who are the stakeholders affected by Jane's action? (stakeholder analysis)
    - ■ Was the action fair? Was the action culturally acceptable? Does the action violate an unspoken promise? (applying ethical theories—Explain to the students how each question applies to an ethical theory)
- • Scenario 2:
  - o Paula and Gail are roommates and currently taking different sections of an intermediate sociology class. Both have an assignment to write a four-page paper that evaluates a research article on the topic of racial tensions in prison. The assignment is due after spring break. Because Paula is going to Florida with friends over break, she completes the paper well in advance of when it is due. Gail has confided in you that she has been struggling with the class and is having difficulty with this particular assignment. After spring break, you and Gail are talking, and you ask her how the assignment went. Gail tells you

that she found a copy of Paula's paper in the recycle bin and that she made a few minor modifications to it and submitted it. Gail doesn't seem remorseful about her actions. You are friends not only with Gail but also with Paula. Neither one of them has received a grade for her paper yet.

- Who are the stakeholders affected by Jane's action? (stakeholder analysis)
- Was the action fair? Was the action culturally acceptable? Does the action violate an unspoken promise?
- What do you do? Discuss the options available to you and be prepared to select one and justify your selection.

The proximity of a situation to an individual does have an impact on how he or she responds to the situation and how unethical he or she finds an act to be. This scenario will often result in interesting discussions because known individuals are involved. It differs slightly from scenarios in which a student submits a paper from a report bank or from the Web. If time permits, present the students with a modified scenario in which Gail is their roommate and she submitted their paper as her own.

Session 3: GVV Workshop—Writing and Presenting Scripts

- Goal: To have students draft a script that allows them to voice their concerns about an unethical action that occurred.
- Teaching strategy: This session is a workshop, so the instructor will provide the framework for the task and then ask students to work in small groups to draft a script that they will later present to the class. The instructor and classmates will provide constructive feedback on tactics that were successful and those that can be modified for more effectiveness.

  The scenario presented can build from the ones presented during session 2, adding continuity and cohesiveness to the sessions. However, the scenario does need to state that the protagonist has decided to take action. The option to do nothing is not available.
- Sample scenario:
  o Paula and Gail are roommates and currently taking different sections of an intermediate sociology class. Both have an assignment to write a four-page paper that evaluates a research article on the topic of racial tensions in prison. The assignment is due after spring break. Because Paula is going to Florida with friends over break, she completes the paper well in advance of when it is due. Gail has confided in another friend, Sally, that she has been struggling with the class and is having difficulty with this particular assignment. After spring break, Gail and Sally are talking, and Gail tells Sally that she found a copy of Paula's paper in the recycle bin and that she made a few minor modifications to it and submitted it. Gail doesn't seem remorseful about her actions. Sally is friends not only with Gail but also with Paula. Neither one of them has received a grade for her paper yet. Sally believes strongly that

students are accountable for their own work and feels that Gail's actions are unfair to Paula, the professor, and the other classmates. Gail is her friend, but Paula is as well. Sally doesn't feel that she can ignore the information she has. Sally knows that she needs to speak up. How should she address the situation? With whom should she speak, and what should she say?

After deciding whom Sally would speak with, draft a script that conveys the conversation she would have with the person.

In this workshop, the scripts will likely be varied. Some students may have the conversation with Gail and discuss why the action is unethical and encourage Gail to remedy the situation. Some students may have the discussion with Paula, who unknowingly was affected by the action, while other students may opt to meet with the professor to convey what they know about the situation.

Introducing the scenario and the tasks will take approximately 10 minutes. Once the students have the assignments, allow them 20 minutes to write their scripts. The final 20 minutes of the class is reserved for the groups to present their scripts and receive feedback. If you have a large class and do not have time for all the scripts to be heard by the entire class, you can have groups pair up and provide peer feedback to one another.

Extracurricular Approach: A 50 Minute Session for a Noncurricular Event, Such as International Student Orientation

In this instruction session, the first 15 to 20 minutes sets context for international students about academic ethics in your university setting by introducing key ethical concepts and tools. The remaining 30 to 35 minutes uses a case-based approach to apply the tools.

- Goal: To acknowledge that the cultural expectations and traditions at your university may be different from the student's home university. Demonstrate what ethical student behavior looks like at your institution.
- Teaching strategy: The first section of the session is a brief overview of ethical concepts and tools. Once the overview is completed, present a scenario and discuss the questions as a group. For the second scenario, break the class into small groups and have them discuss a scenario and prepare a three-minute summary to share with the larger group.
- Main points to cover:
  - o Definition of ethics and why people behave ethically
    - Set of beliefs about right and wrong and using those beliefs to guide decisions
    - Examples of why people behave ethically—avoids harm to others, builds trust, reciprocity (Golden Rule), and avoids risk of damaging their reputation or their organization's reputation

o Ethical concepts
  ▪ Theoretical criteria
  ▪ Practical criteria
    • For usual standards—reference Student Code of Conduct section on academic integrity
o Plagiarism/academic misconduct scenarios
  ▪ Scenario 1 (facilitate large-group discussion):
    Susan finds a flash drive in a computer at the library. While trying to identify the owner, she notices that the owner took the same biology course that she is currently taking. The course is assignment intensive with many labs and short papers. She has a lab report due this week, and this has been particularly challenging and is about 50 percent completed. When she looks at the report the owner wrote for this particular lab, she thinks it is much better. Knowing that it would take her another two hours to complete her own lab report, she decides to submit the report that she found on the flash drive.
    • Apply theoretical and practical criteria to the scenario.
    • Would this act be ethical in your home culture? Why or why not?
    • Would this act be ethical at [university]? Why or why not?
  ▪ Scenario (small-group discussion with three-minute presentation to larger group)
    Karen is a third-year law student and is submitting a paper to a prestigious competition in which the winner and the school receive national recognition. Her topic is international adoption. Using Lexis and Westlaw, Karen finds articles on her topic. She takes five articles and cuts and pastes the content and footnotes from these articles to assemble a paper.
  ▪ Apply theoretical and practical criteria to the scenario.
  ▪ Would this act be ethical in your home culture? Why or why not?
  ▪ Would this act be ethical at [university]? Why or why not?

The models and sample curricula presented above demonstrate ways in which ethics can be incorporated into plagiarism instruction. As you prepare your sessions, identify the objectives and goals of the session. Is the purpose of the session to raise awareness that plagiarism is an ethical issue? To have students analyze an issue to determine if the action is unethical? To have students begin discussing their role in an attempt to combat plagiarism and change the culture of plagiarism as an acceptable behavior? The goals and objectives of the session will influence which models are used. As with all instruction, it is important to incorporate an assessment component to help determine whether the session was successful in achieving the objectives defined. We discuss assessment strategies in chapters 6 and 7.

NOTES

1. R. Edward Freeman, *Strategic Management: A Stakeholder Approach* (Boston: Pitman, 1984).

2. R. Eric Reidenbach and Donald P. Robin, "Toward the Development of a Multidimensional Scale for Improving Evaluations of Business Ethics," *Journal of Business Ethics* 9, no. 8 (1990): 639–53, http://www.jstor.org/stable/25072080.

3. Jane Mallor, A. James Barnes, L. Thomas Bowers, and Arlen Lanvardt, *Business Law: The Ethical, Global, and E-Commerce Environment* (Boston: McGraw-Hill, 2006); David P. Twomey, Marianne M. Jennings, and Stephanie M. Greene, *Anderson's Business Law and the Legal Environment, Comprehensive Volume* (Boston: Cengage Learning, 2016).

4. W. Michael Hoffman and Robert E. McNulty, "A Business Ethics Theory of Whistleblowing: Responding to the $1 Trillion Question," in *Whistleblowing: In Defense of Proper Action*, ed. Marek Arszulowicz and Wojciech W. Gasparski (New Brunswick, NJ: Transaction, 2011), 45–59; Robert A. Harris, *The Plagiarism Handbook: Strategies for Preventing, Detecting and Dealing with Plagiarism* (Los Angeles: Pyrczak Publishing, 2001), 150–52.

5. Mary C. Gentile, *Giving Voice to Values: How to Speak Your Mind When You Know What's Right* (New Haven, CT: Yale University Press, 2010).

6. Harris, *The Plagiarism Handbook*, 151.

7. Freeman, *Strategic Management*, 25.

8. David Lyons, "Utilitarianism," in *Blackwell Encyclopedic Dictionary of Business Ethics*, ed. Patricia Hogue Werhane and R. Edward Freeman (Malden, MA: Wiley, 1998), 640–44, http://search.ebscohost.com/login.aspx?direct=true&db=nlebk&AN=45053&site=ehost-livea.

9. Jean M. Twenge, W. Keith Campbell, and Elise C. Freeman, "Generational Differences in Young Adults' Life Goals, Concern for Others and Civic Orientation, 1966–2009," *Journal of Personality and Social Psychology* 102, no. 5 (2012): 1058, https://www.apa.org/pubs/journals/releases/psp-102-5-1045.pdf.

10. Brook J. Sadler, "The Wrongs of Plagiarism: Ten Quick Arguments," *Teaching Philosophy* 30, no. 3 (2007): 283–91, http://www.pdcnet.org/scholarpdf/show?id=teachphil_2007_0030_0003_0283_0291&pdfname=teachphil_2007_0030_0003_0283_0291.pdf&file_type=pdf.

11. Ibid., 284.

12. Ibid., 285.

13. Ibid., 287.

14. Rafik Z. Elias and Neung J. Kim, "The Relationship between Accounting Students' Perceptions of Cheating Behavior and Questionable Workplace Behavior," *Central Business Review* 24, no. 1–2 (2005): 16–19, doi:10.1007/s10805-011-9144-1; Randi L. Sims, "The Relationship between Academic Dishonesty and Unethical Business Practices," *Journal of Education for Business* 68, no. 4 (1993): 207–11, doi:10.1080/08832323.1993.10117614; Raef A. Lawson, "Is Classroom Cheating Related to Business Students' Propensity to Cheat in the 'Real World'?," *Journal of Business Ethics* 49, no. 2 (2004): 189–99, doi:10.1023/B:BUSI.0000015784.34148.cb; Sarath Nonis and Cathy Owens Swift, "An Examination of the Relationship between Academic Dishonesty and Workplace Dishonesty: A Multicampus Investigation," *Journal of Education for Business* 77, no. 2 (2001): 69–77, doi:10.1016/j.paid.2007.03.017.

15. Sadler, "The Wrongs of Plagiarism," 286.

16. Ibid., 288.

17. Reidenbach and Robin, "Toward the Development of a Multidimensional Scale for Improving Evaluations of Business Ethics."

18. Cheryl A. Cruz, William E. Shafer, and Jerry R. Strawser, "A Multidimensional Analysis of Tax Practitioners' Ethical Judgments," *Journal of Business Ethics* 24, no. 3 (2000): 223–44, doi:10.1023/A:1006140809998; Simon Hudson and Graham Miller, "Ethical Orientation and Awareness of Tourism Students," *Journal of Business Ethics* 62, no. 4 (2005): 383–96, doi:10.1007/s10551-005-0850-8; Insung Jung, "Ethical Judgments and Behaviors: Applying a Multidimensional Ethics Scale to Measuring ICT Ethics of College Students," *Computers and Education* 53, no. 3 (2009): 940–49, doi:10.1016/j.compedu.2009.05.011.

19. Jung, "Ethical Judgments and Behaviors"; Shu Ching Yang, "Ethical Academic Judgments and Behaviors: Applying a Multidimensional Ethics Scale to Measure the Ethical Academic Behavior of Graduate Students," *Ethics and Behavior* 22, no. 4 (2012): 281–96, http://www.tandfonline.com/doi/pdf/10.1080/10508422.2012.672907; Connie Strittmatter and Virginia K. Bratton, "Plagiarism Awareness among Students: Assessing Integration of Ethics Theory into Library Instruction." *College & Research Libraries* 75, no. 5 (2014): 736–52, http://crl.acrl.org/content/75/5/736.short.

20. Reidenbach and Robin, "Toward the Development of a Multidimensional Scale for Improving Evaluations of Business Ethics," 645.

21. Ibid., 646.

22. Ibid., 647.

23. Mallor et al., *Business Law*; Twomey et al., *Anderson's Business Law and the Legal Environment, Comprehensive Volume.*

24. Reidenbach and Robin, "Toward the Development of a Multidimensional Scale for Improving Evaluations of Business Ethics," 645.

25. Harris, *The Plagiarism Handbook*, 150–52.

26. Hoffman and McNulty, "A Business Ethics Theory of Whistleblowing," 51.

27. Ibid.

28. Gentile, *Giving Voice to Values.*

29. Olusegun Agboola Sogunro, "Efficacy of Role-Playing Pedagogy in Training Leaders: Some Reflections," *Journal of Management Development* 23, no. 4 (2004): 356, http://dx.doi.org/10.1108/02621710410529802; Ulrika Westrup and Agneta Planander, "Role-Play as a Pedagogical Method to Prepare Students for Practice: The Students' Voice, *Hogre Utbildning* 3, no. 3 (2013): 204, http://journals.lub.lu.se/index.php/hus/article/view/5609/8155.

30. Harris, *The Plagiarism Handbook*, 35–36.

5

Putting It into Action

Implementing Plagiarism and Ethics Awareness Training in the Classroom

In the previous chapter, we discussed the content to be delivered during a Plagiarism and Ethics Awareness Training (PEAT) session. Now that you are armed with the content and types of exercises that can be used, we turn our attention on how to effectively present this training within diverse environments. When implementing the PEAT curriculum, there are several issues the instructor must address that can be further complicated based on whether the instructor is the primary instructor for the class or a guest lecturer. As the primary instructor for the class, you will have a lot of flexibility in designing the amount of time dedicated to the topic, evaluating the effectiveness of the instruction, designing assignments to reinforce the course content, and grading activities used in the curriculum.

We recognize that in most instances, the librarian will be a guest instructor. As a guest instructor, you will have to work closely with the primary instructor to obtain buy-in to the curriculum. Some suggestions to ensure that the integrity of the curriculum is maintained include the following:

- Requiring the instructor to be present during the session: We rarely agree to do a PEAT session without the instructor being present. First, having the instructor in the classroom sends a message to students that this is an important topic and not just a filler topic to be used when the instructor has a conflict and needs to miss class. This is similar to requiring that a traditional library instruction session is tied to a research assignment so that the session is a meaningful experience for students. Second, if the instructor is present and understands the content being taught, he or she can continue to tie in the information throughout the remainder of the course. Finally, the presence of the classroom instructor helps with classroom management. With the instructor present, students are less likely to walk out of class and be disruptive and are more likely to participate.[1]

• Incorporating assessment or graded component: Ideally, you do not want your PEAT session to be one where you present the curriculum and nothing further happens. Work with the instructor to see whether you can do a pre/postsurvey to evaluate whether the session had an impact on students' ethical perceptions of an act of plagiarism (see chapters 6 and 7 for more information on pre/post-surveys). Pre/postsurveys are helpful because they engage students in the topic before and after you present the curriculum. Students are required to grapple with the content multiple times, reinforcing the content delivered during the PEAT session. An instructor can make pre/postsurvey a graded assignment in which they award points for completing the survey (not for how the questions are answered).[2] If possible, work with the primary instructor to have activities associated with the session included in part of their overall grade for the course. If teaching in an online or in-person environment, you and the instructor could assign points for participation in the discussion or role-playing activities. Alternatively, students could be assigned to write a short essay after the session to reflect on the content, discussion, and activities covered in the PEAT session.

When presenting the PEAT session as a guest instructor, we have achieved the most success by having the primary instructor allow us to do the pre/postsurvey. Our overarching premise is that by increasing student awareness that plagiarism is an ethical issue, we hope to see a reduction of academic misconduct. When we meet with the instructor, we discuss how plagiarism avoidance is currently taught and how our approach to plagiarism avoidance provides a different perspective (focusing on the ethicality of the issue rather than the mechanics of how to attribute correctly). We also discuss the relationship between college misconduct and workplace misconduct. After one or two instructors agreed to do the pre/postsurvey, we were able to persuade other instructors to participate because we were able to demonstrate that the instruction session had an impact on students' ethical perceptions of plagiarism-related issues.

The remaining portion of this chapter discusses techniques for successful implementation of the PEAT curriculum regardless of whether the instructor is the primary instructor or a guest instructor. We focus on effective strategies for a successful classroom discussion and role playing, which are the primary techniques used in the curriculum. In addition, we discuss how to effectively implement the curriculum in more challenging situations, such as large classes (50 or more students) and the online environment. Finally, we provide some suggestions on how to deal with difficult personalities you may face in the classroom.

LEADING EFFECTIVE CLASS DISCUSSIONS

In chapter 3, we outlined why case-based problem discussions are a valid pedagogical tool to use when discussing the ethicality of plagiarism. Instead of students receiving a lecture about why plagiarism is unethical, students are tasked with determining whether an action is unethical. Discussion requires students to engage with and debate the issues associated with academic integrity. It requires them to critically think about the issues and come to a logical conclusion. During the process, students not only discuss their viewpoints but also critically listen and respond to their classmates' comments. In chapter 4, we presented several different models that can be used to facilitate the discussion. Students are presented with a scenario, and carefully crafted questions are used as prompts to imitate the discussion. However, leading a discussion requires more than presenting a question prompt and letting students comment. There is an underlying structure to the discussion, and as the instructor, you have several tasks to ensure that the discussion is successful in achieving its objectives.

The PEAT model relies heavily on student participation. Effectively moderating a class discussion to ensure student participation is important. As an instructor, your role in problem-based case discussions is to serve as the facilitator. This role requires a critical balance between guiding and monopolizing—you want to guide the conversation so that important points are discussed but avoid monopolizing the conversation to the point where students' contributions are stymied. At the start of the discussion, you will need to set the stage and provide context for the discussion. Explain the format of the discussion. In our PEAT experience, the average class size was 45 or more students. With this size of class, discussions were more effective when we broke the class into small groups to discuss the scenario and questions and then followed with a debriefing session for the class as a whole. However, if the class size is small (fewer than 20 students), you may decide to have an overall class discussion and forgo the small groups. Consider which discussion model will lead to increased student participation and engagement for your particular class.

Lay out the ground rules for the discussion. Ask students to actively listen to their classmates' comments even if they differ from their own viewpoints. Students should keep an open mind and withhold judgment until all sides of an issue have been presented. Avoid interrupting one another and keep to the topic at hand. If a student wants to introduce a new topic, he or she should wait until the current topic ends naturally. Address the smaller logistical issue of whether students need to raise their hands in order to speak. If you are a guest speaker, you may want them to create a name card so that you can easily call a person by name as opposed to pointing to people to speak.[3]

Introduce the problem and questions that need to be answered. We project the scenario and questions on the screen in the classroom so that students can easily refer back to them. An alternative is to create a handout for each group or student. If having students break into small groups, ask them to delegate a student to report the outcomes of their discussion to the class during the debriefing session and to write out their answers on a sheet of paper to be turned in at the end of class. This holds them accountable for answering the questions in their small groups rather than turning the allotted discussion time into an opportunity to discuss other topics.

The facilitator also has to guide the discussion by synthesizing points made during the discussion, clarifying student comments, and expanding on points that were raised.[4] Through this process, an active learning environment is created in which students explore the scenario from various viewpoints. As a facilitator, you need to listen carefully to what students are saying. Students value when you take time to acknowledge their comments by providing nonverbal cues, such as making eye contact or nodding.[5] If possible, you may want to take mental or written notes so that you can summarize the conversation or refer back to a discussion point at a later time.[6] As you listen to students' comments, you may need to intervene periodically to help keep the conversation going. Avoid stating your opinion, as that may shut down the discussion. However, you do not need to remain silent during the discussion. There are several types of questions that you can ask to further the conversation:

- Justifying questions are used when a student provides an answer but does not explain why he or she selected it.[7] For example, if a student responds to a scenario and states that he or she would not report a known instance of plagiarism, the facilitator could ask, "What are the implications for not reporting the plagiarism violation?" or "Why do you feel that the plagiarism incident does not need to be reported?"
- Clarifying questions are used when a student does not fully answer a question or the comment is unclear.[8] If a student states that he or she would report an incident of plagiarism because it impacts him or her, the facilitator could ask, "How does the plagiarism incident impact you?"
- Extending questions ask students to think about an extension of the scenario and how it might affect their answers.[9] For example, if a student states that he or she would not report an incident of plagiarism because he or she is not directly affected, the facilitator could ask, "What if the paper were graded on a curve? How might you be impacted then?"

At the end of the class session, provide some closure to the scenario. The wrap-up can include reviewing the issues discussed, answering any outstanding questions, or presenting the correct answer to the scenario if there is one.[10] If planning to provide an assessment of the instruction session, you can inform students about the next steps and when they can expect to receive a survey or other method of evaluation.

LEADING AN EFFECTIVE ROLE-PLAYING ACTIVITY

In chapter 3, we discussed the benefits of role playing as a pedagogical technique for active learning. Role playing puts students into situations that may be new to them. Because they are actively experiencing a situation rather than passively receiving information, as is the case in a lecture or film viewing, an opportunity is presented for students to modify or adapt a previously held attitude.[11] We also discussed why we adopted the Giving Voice to Values (GVV) model. Giving students role-play scenarios in which the characters have already decided that they would address an issue of plagiarism can be a freeing experience for students. The decision-making aspect of the ethical dilemma has been removed for them. Students do not have to worry about how their peers would perceive them if they arrived at that decision on their own accord. The only thing students have to do is prepare and present how they would have the difficult conversation. In chapter 4, we discussed how to present the GVV model during an instruction session. Now we turn our attention to the execution of the role-playing activity. Role play is a powerful tool, so it is important that the activity is well structured.

Facilitating the Role-Playing Activity

Some students may be reluctant to participate in a role-playing activity because they are uncomfortable presenting in front of others. To help alleviate some of their anxieties, discuss with them some of the fears they may be experiencing. They may be surprised and comforted to know that they are not the only ones who are apprehensive about the role play.[12] You can also lay some ground rules for when the group debriefs after the role playing. You do not want students to be overly harsh and critical when they provide feedback, especially if the individual receiving the feedback is already self-conscious about the role-playing activity. Discuss with students the best way to provide feedback. This may include the following:

- Focusing comments on what they actually saw and heard rather than making an assumption based on what they saw and heard (Example: "When talking to the student, your voice was very soft and sounded apologetic" versus "You must really dislike confrontations.")
- Commenting on the action and not the individual (Example: "During the role play, some of your actions like when you hovered over the student were very assertive" versus "You were a bully.")
- Offer specific suggestions rather than generalizations (Example: "You maintained eye contact when confronting the student and held your ground when he or she tried to dismiss your arguments" versus "You were really convincing.")
- Avoid being judgmental (Example: "That was really bad. You weren't convincing at all" versus "You may want to develop your argument regarding the impact on classmates a little bit more to make it more compelling.")[13]

A common role-play approach often referred to as the "fishbowl" technique is to have the students role-play in the front of the room as if on a stage with an audience.[14] Benefits to this method are that you and all of the students are able to provide feedback to the student's role play and that everyone has the opportunity to see how role plays varied. However, this is a time-consuming process, and the repetition of role plays will likely cause students to become bored and disengaged. An alternative technique is to break the class into smaller groups and have several role plays occur simultaneously. In small groups, each student does his or her role play and receives feedback from his or her group. At the end of class, everyone can come together to debrief and share highlights of their interactions. As you can imagine, the advantages and disadvantages of this model are the opposite of the fishbowl technique. The richness of the feedback is diminished because students can receive feedback only from the group members and do not have the benefit of everyone's feedback. In addition, you, as the instructor, will not get to see every student's role play, so some may miss out on your feedback. Aside from saving time and reducing potential boredom and disengagement, an additional benefit to running simultaneous role plays is the reduction of student anxiety. Because students are not on the center stage, they are likely to be less embarrassed and may feel safer conducting their role play within a smaller group and with other activity occurring around them.[15]

We recommend using the small-group model for role play largely because you will likely be facing some significant time constraints and want to ensure that everyone has a chance to practice their role plays.

Debriefing after the Role Playing

While it is easy to get caught up in the role-playing activities, you want to make sure that you leave adequate time toward the end of class for a debriefing discussion. Thiagarajan identified six questions, or components, that can be included during a debriefing conversation:[16]

- How do you feel?[17] During the debriefing session, students can reflect on how they felt addressing the plagiarism issue to the professor or perpetrator and their reactions to other role plays that they witnessed. This question solicits students' emotional responses to the role-playing activity.
- What happened?[18] After students have talked about how they felt during the role play, you can delve a bit further and inquire about strategies that worked well for them and those that weren't as effective. This question allows students to decouple from the role-playing activity and take a more analytical look at the approach they used.[19]
- What did you learn?[20] This question allows students to begin brainstorming ways to make their role plays more effective. If a student says that a tactic he or she tried didn't work very well, you can ask the class how it might be modified to be more effective. You can also ask students if they heard something in another's role play that they thought was particularly compelling that they might want to adopt in their own.
- How does this relate to the real world?[21] The purpose of the role-playing activity is to provide students with practice addressing a realistic situation that they may encounter. You can query students about whether they feel that the role play was realistic and translatable to a real-world experience. If not, ask them how they could make it so that what they practiced today could be executable in a real situation.

- What if?[22] Present students with alternate scenarios. What would have happened if the person you were confronting responded this way? This helps students prepare for any curveball that they may receive if confronted with a situation in which they need to address an ethical plagiarism violation.
- What next?[23] This question moves role play from simulated environment to reality. You can ask them how they would react in a real-world situation. Would they be more comfortable confronting the person, or would they opt to say nothing? You can also ask how they can continue to further prepare themselves in case they find themselves in a situation similar to the role-play scenario.

Role playing is an effective active learning tool that can help prepare students for encounters in which they are witness to plagiarism violations. For role play to be effective, there needs to be sufficient time to execute the activity. Therefore, we recommend that role play be used when you are the primary instructor for a class and can dedicate the appropriate time to it. If you are a guest, you will need to have several class sessions dedicated to presenting the PEAT curriculum. We do not recommend using role play if you have only one class session to present the PEAT material.

ONLINE TEACHING

While the curriculum described in chapter 4 focused mainly on in-person instruction, it can also be tailored to an online course. Instruction in online settings comes with its challenges as well as advantages. For example, online interactions may feel impersonal and less engaging to some students. However, other students who feel less comfortable speaking out in class may find it easier to participate in an online setting. We explore these challenges and benefits in the following paragraphs.

Online Discussions

Because much of online discussion is asynchronous, it can be challenging to create an environment in which meaningful dialogue is exchanged. When preparing an assignment that contains an online discussion component, the design of the discussion topic is important. A discussion forum can ask students to generate exam questions, solve a problem, debate an issue, examine a case, or answer a question prompt in which students need to make substantive replies to their classmates. In any of these scenarios, the instructor needs to ensure that the question or task presented is focused and clear so that students have a framework in which they can work.[24]

When presenting the PEAT curriculum in an online environment, we often use the stakeholder analysis and theoretical criteria modules. We use these models because students are presented with focused, specific questions that pertain to real-life experiences. Prior to the discussion, we either create an online presentation or prepare a handout to explain what stakeholder analysis is and how the three questions

(Was the action fair? Is the action culturally acceptable? Does the action violate an unwritten contract?) relate to ethical theory. The discussion assignment has three components. First, students have to post their responses addressing the stakeholder analysis and theoretical criteria questions. At this point, we do not let students see their classmates' posts because we do not want them to regurgitate what has previously been said. Once they make their first post, they can see the online discussion. Second, students must provide a meaningful comment to one of their classmates. Finally, students must reply to a comment that a classmate made on their postings. This three-pronged approach follows closely with the recommendations outlined in Rovai's article for creating effective online discussion.[25] By requiring students to post three meaningful comments, a sense of community is created, facilitating engaging dialogue among students.

The size of the online class will determine whether you have one forum or whether you need to subdivide the class to create multiple forums. Too few students can stymie discussions because of a lack of interaction. Because the discussions occur in an asynchronous environment, gaining traction on the discussion topics may be difficult because of the time lag between responses. Too many students in a discussion can lead to an overwhelming number of responses for students to read and respond to.[26] In a large forum, a student may make a meaningful and significant comment, only to find that no one responded to it. The owners of these "orphaned comments"[27] may become disengaged and cease contributing to the discussion. Some research suggests that the ideal number of student participants in an online forum is between four and 12 and never to exceed 20.[28] Other research suggests that 20 to 39 students is the maximum.[29] We generally will create discussion forums containing 10 to 12 students.

For students to have a successful online discussion, the instructor needs to provide students with the ground rules for the discussion and establish clear expectations for what is considered an acceptable post. As instructors, we cannot assume that students understand what constitutes a meaningful and substantive comment. A discussion rubric is a useful tool that an instructor can provide to students to ensure that they understand what is expected of them. Not only does it provide them with the guidelines to be successful in the discussion, but it also encourages students to reflect on their discussion responses. When students compare their responses to the criteria outlined in the rubric, they are evaluating their written content and become judges of their work.[30] When we design a rubric, we assign the points allocated for each level of response so that students are fully aware of the grade they will receive in relation to the effort made.

An instructor can also provide clear instruction so that students understand how they should post their responses. Students should support any opinions expressed in a post with data or evidence, which can include personal experiences. While most learning management systems allow for threaded discussions, we encourage students to use descriptive subject lines so that others know specifically which point the student is addressing in the online discussion. Provide feedback. If everyone is contributing thoughtful comments and there is a genuine exchange of ideas, post on their forum to let the students know they are doing well. If the responses are lacking in content, ask pointed questions in the forum to encourage students to expand on their original comments.[31]

Ensuring student participation can be more challenging in an online environment than in a face-to-face environment because the discussions are asynchronous. Students are popping in and out of the discussion as their time permits. While the goal of the group discussion is to have student-to-student interaction, a complete lack of an instructor's presence can lead to stalled discussions. Students may feel that their comments, in which they put significant time and effort, have fallen into an abyss. To keep students engaged in the discussion and to let them know that you are following the discussion, an instructor should post at least once a day to help focus the discussion if it is going off topic and ask thought-provoking or clarifying questions to help stimulate discussion.[32]

Online Role Playing

Role playing can also be used in an online environment. Many of the techniques described in the section "Leading an Effective Role-Playing Activity" are applicable. This section focuses on the execution of the role-play activity in an online environment. Due to the asynchronous nature of online classes and the time commitments required for online role playing, we would recommend that this be used only if you are the primary instructor for a credited class and can dedicate a week or two for the role-playing activity.

A limited amount of research has been conducted on online role playing. Bender discusses several strategies for asynchronous online role playing.[33] She breaks students into groups for a role-playing activity and creates a discussion forum where they can meet and prepare for their role play. When students are set to act out their role play, a new forum is created for the group to present their scenario to non–group members. A separate discussion board is created for the entire class to discuss and analyze the role play. Bender uses this technique in an ethics course and literary analysis class.

Ludewig and Ludewig-Rowher[34] use in-house-constructed simulation software for groups to role-play historical events occurring in East and West Germany during the 1960s and 1970s. Students are assigned roles and are asked to remain in character during the course of the simulation. Students can view materials and are given assignments to act out in character. The majority of the simulation is done asynchronously, but students are required to attend two synchronous sessions each week.

If thinking about using role playing for a GVV scenario, you could consider asking students to use video for their role play. Students would need to work independently and solicit the help of a friend or family member to assume the role of the person they are confronting. Given that smartphones have video capability and the relative ease of creating videos, students could record their role play and post it to their course site. You can assign groups and ask students to review the video posted within their group and provide feedback. The discussion and feedback portion of the role-play exercise could be done through a discussion forum (asynchronous) or through the chat feature in the learning management system (synchronous).

TEACHING A LARGE CLASS

The PEAT method can be more challenging to apply in a large class (more than 50 students), but it is doable. We have done PEAT sessions in classes with 90 students and more than 120 students. Typically, we use the stakeholder analysis and theoretical and practical criteria modules. Due to the size of the class, we do not recommend using role play as a tool in these sessions. As you can imagine, the challenges with large-class instruction are maintaining student engagement and facilitating meaningful discussion. In a large class, students often feel anonymous and as a result feel less personal responsibility to be active contributors to the class.[35] Large-class instruction is often associated with transmissive teaching, which, as discussed in chapter 3, results in students receiving information passively rather than interacting with the course content. Primary instructors are challenged to connect with students in a large class on a meaningful level. As a guest instructor in a large class, it is likely that you will struggle to achieve meaningful connections with the bulk of the students. However, that does not mean that you cannot provide effective instruction or an engaging class session that results in meaningful discussions.

Small-Group Discussion

As with a small class, you can break students into small groups to discuss a topic. To hear comments from all of the groups, you may want to try the snowball technique.[36] For example, if teaching a class of 120 students, break the students into groups of three (40 groups) and ask them to complete the stakeholder analysis and theoretical criteria modules. Give them five minutes to discuss and write their responses. After the time is up, have each group pair with another group (six students in 20 groups) for another five minutes. Ask them to consolidate their responses and add to the list. You can have them merge one more time (12 students in 10 groups) and repeat the process. After 15 to 20 minutes, students have had three rounds of discussion about the plagiarism scenario. Ideally, as the groups grow, students will hear new approaches that spark additional discussion. Ask each group to provide a one-minute summary of what they find and finish the class with an open forum discussion. As the groups debrief, make note of the differences you hear among groups and use that to facilitate the larger group discussion. For example, if two groups respond differently to a scenario question that asks what a student would do if he or she knew that an act of plagiarism was committed, you can use that as a springboard for discussion. Question the groups about why they agree or disagree with the other group's answer.

One of the benefits to the snowball technique is that every student does contribute to the discussion. At the very least, a student should be contributing to the initial round of discussion involving two or three students. As the groups come together, they may hear some opinions that differ from theirs that can lead to further discussion. However, we recognize that participation by each individual student is likely to decrease due to the increasing size of the group. And while we hope that each group brings something unique to the discussion, students may feel that the groups are repetitive if there is a lack of diversity in group answers. However, keeping each group meeting to five minutes should keep the groups moving so that students do not feel that there is a lot of downtime.

Using Technology in a Large Classroom

To accompany large-group discussion, you can also incorporate personal response systems (e.g., clickers) into questions to help stimulate discussion. Clickers can be used to ensure that all students participate, and because responses are anonymous, students are more likely to respond and may answer questions honestly rather than how they think they ought to answer.[37] Clickers lend themselves nicely to the theoretical criteria module. For example, when students are presented with the scenario, they are asked to rate how fair the action was on a scale of 1 to 10, with 1 being unfair and 10 being totally fair. When using clickers, the scale will need to be adjusted to 1 to 5 given that clickers allow for only five choices. When students provide their ratings, you can quickly gauge how they responded and then begin a discussion on why they responded the way they did. Because students had to make a selection, they have given some thought to the question, making them more willing to share in a discussion.

Not all large classes require their students to purchase clickers. There are many free or low-cost online polling sites that allow students to respond to questions via their smartphones. Students are presented with a questions, and they text their answers to a number. The polling code can be embedded into a PowerPoint presentation so that you can project the question. One caveat to using these tools for open-ended questions is students can type any reply they want, so you may have some students who want to be funny and submit replies that are not related to the question at hand. As an instructor, you can have a little bit of fun with this, but you need to keep it in check. If the responses get out of hand, you can quickly lose control of your class. One way to handle this is to simply turn off the projector so that the answers do not appear on the screen for the students to see. The answers will still appear on your monitor, and you can parse out the serious responses from the flippant ones and continue the discussion with minimal disruption.

STUDENT PERSONALITIES IN THE CLASSROOM

Whether you are a guest instructor or a primary instructor for the course, you are bound to run into situations in which the classroom activities are not progressing as well as you had hoped. This is especially challenging and exasperating when the majority of the class content is contingent on student participation. Below are some suggested strategies for handling the diverse student personality types that you will inevitably face at some point during your teaching career.

The Quiet Student

Many of us have experienced that sinking feeling when a question is posed to a class and you hear nothing but crickets. Your well-designed, carefully crafted question is met with blank stares and awkward silence. These prolonged silences can feel like your worst enemy. A lack of student participation can occur for many reasons, including apathy, embarrassment, or overall passiveness:[38]

- Apathetic student: Apathy can be addressed by providing interesting topics. Typically, students enjoy discussing incidents of plagiarism because it deviates from traditional plagiarism instruction, which is more mechanical and structured.
- Embarrassed student: Overcoming the fear of embarrassment usually occurs as students get to know one another and become more comfortable talking with one another. If you are a guest instructor, you will not likely be able to change student behaviors in a class session, but you may try scheduling the class session later in the semester in hopes that students are more familiar with one another. Prior to the class session, you may want to consult with the primary instructor to learn about the dynamics of the class so that you can be prepared when you come to teach. Once in the classroom, you can be encouraging and nonjudgmental when asking students for their thoughts.
- Passive students: Passive students are often a result of their learning environment. Their passiveness is understandable if they have been only in classes in which transmissive learning occurs. Students may not be comfortable sharing and discussing issues because they have never been expected to participate.[39]

If you have a quiet class that is not responding to any questions, ask the students a question and have them write on a sheet of paper how they would rate the issue on a scale of 1 to 10. As you progress through the ratings, have the students raise their hands if they scored it that number. You can then call on a student or two who scored the scenario differently and ask him or her to explain why he or she gave the scenario that rating.[40] Sometimes it takes students time to acclimate, so while silence is uncomfortable, it is often a necessary part of discussion. If you ask a question and do not receive an immediate answer, let there be silence. Students may be processing the question or may be challenging you to see if you will give them the answer. Usually, if you wait long enough, a student will respond.[41]

The Talkative Student

In some cases, when you present your well-crafted question, you may have an initial pause, but then a hand raises, and a student starts to speak. You feel relief. The conversation has started. While initially you may be thrilled to have one or two students contributing to the conversation, you quickly realize that what should be a broad discussion among a class of 30 is becoming a two-way conversation. Your one or two actively engaged students are monopolizing the conversation. Some students may be happy to have a classmate monopolize the conversation, but more often than not, it becomes annoying for the other students who may want to contribute but have a difficult time inserting themselves into the conversation.[42] If you notice that the conversation is being dominated by one or two students, you can make a statement like, "We have heard some very interesting points by Sue and John. Thank you. I am curious to hear what other people think about the actions that Jane took in the scenario we reviewed." Another strategy is to break the class into smaller groups, and having each group debrief to the entire class is another way to help ensure that multiple voices are heard.

The Rude Student

As a guest instructor, it can be very difficult to figure out how to handle students who are behaving poorly in the classroom. The rude student can assume many identities: the student who is sleeping in the back of the class, two students who are chatting with one another while the instructor or another student is talking, or the student who is texting on his or her phone during class. Ideally, you will have the help of the primary instructor in handling these situations, but in cases where the instructor is not present or not willing to address the situation, you need to do what you can to ensure that the instruction session stays on track.

Student misbehavior is not a personal reflection on you. More often than not, the behavior has been exhibited during other classroom sessions and has not been addressed appropriately by the primary instructor. In addition, the primary instructor may not have properly prepared the students for your arrival, so they may not understand how the PEAT session relates to their course work. In the latter instance, you can begin the class by explaining why you are there and the objectives of the classroom session and how they relate either to the class or, more broadly, to their academic careers.

The one theme that all of the characteristics of the rude student have in common is that they are not engaged in the class activities. To get them to cease their disruptive behavior, you want to find a balance between not embarrassing them and demonstrating that you are serious in your request of asking them to pay attention.

At the beginning of the class session, you will likely introduce the material and activities for the class. Take this time to survey the classroom to identify those students who may be disengaged. If you plan to break the class into small groups, there are a couple of strategies that you can use:

- Assign groups rather than have students self-select their groups: Have students count off from 1 to 5 to create their group. All of the 1s are a group, all of the 2s are a group, and so on. This can serve two purposes. First, it will break up groups of students who are friends and more likely to conduct side conversations during class. They will be separated for the duration of the class. Second, it will get people up and moving. This may rejuvenate the sleeping students and will likely move them from the back of the classroom to the front. This approach will take longer to get groups established but will likely be worth it in the long run.
- Assign disruptive students a task: Once small groups are established, go to each group and assign the disengaged students a task, such as reporting the results of the small group, taking notes for the group, or taking the lead in the role-playing session. Asking them to take on an active role will likely increase their engagement.

During a classwide discussion or role-playing activity, try to be mobile. Move about the classroom. If you notice that a student is sleeping, texting, or talking to another, you can casually approach him or her while other students are participating in the class conversation. Simply standing near them or pointing to the phone can let students know that they need to cease their activity. For students who are having side conversations during the class, you can ask them if they would like to contribute. For example, "Did you have something you wanted to add to the conversation?" If they answer no, then you can say, "I would just ask that your conversation be related to content that contributes to the class discussion."

The goal of this chapter on implementation is to provide you with a starting point for the successful implementation of the PEAT curriculum that can be incorporated into a number of learning environments. All elements are conducive to in-person classes of 50 or fewer students. Many elements are conducive for online courses and large classes. Because active learning techniques are used that, in essence, put the class in the hands of the students, effectively implementing the curriculum requires commitment and preparation. The preparation for teaching in an active learning environment is different from preparing a presentation in which you control the pace and content delivered. When preparing to teach using discussions or role play, you need to anticipate potential problems (lack of participation, challenging students, etc.). You need to have a solid understanding of the content and anticipate issues that may emerge from the activity. A portion of your preparation work will be done in real time—critically listening to student responses so that you can address, clarify, and synthesize issues. In addition, you will need to insert teaching points at appropriate times during the discussions. These are skills that are learnable but that require practice to improve technique.

NOTES

1. Heidi Blackburn and Lauren Hays, "Classroom Management and the Librarian," *Education Libraries* 37, no. 1–2 (2014): 28, http://digitalcommons.unomaha.edu/crisslibfac-pub/11, accessed February 14, 2016.

2. If you are planning on publishing results of the pre/postsurveys, you may not be able to make them a required assignment. Some institutional review boards will frown on requiring students to complete a survey and ask that you make an alternate assignment available to students so that they can opt out. However, instructors can offer incentive-like bonus points if students complete the survey.

3. Barbara Gross Davis, *Tools for Teaching* (Hoboken, NJ: Jossey-Bass, 2009), 98–99.

4. Jay Alden and Judith Kirkhorn, "Case Studies," in *The ASTD Training and Development Handbook*, ed. Robert L. Craig (New York: McGraw-Hill, 1996), 506.

5. Marilla D. Svinicki and Wilbert J. McKeachie, *McKeachie's Teaching Tips: Strategies, Research and Theory for College and University Teachers* (Belmont, CA: Cengage Learning, 2014), 46.

6. Davis, *Tools for Teaching*, 101.

7. Kate Exley and Reg Dennick, *Small Group Teaching: Tutorials, Seminars and Beyond* (New York: Routledge Falmer, 2004), 45.

8. Ibid.

9. Ibid.

10. Alden and Kirkhorn, "Case Studies," 508.

11. Morry van Ments, *The Effective Use of Role-Play: Practical Techniques for Improving Learning* (London: Kogan Page, 1999), 10–11.

12. Ana Lazar, "Setting the Stage: Role-Playing in the Group Work Classroom," *Social Work with Groups* 37, no. 3 (2014): 237, http://dx.doi.org/10.1080/01609513.862894.

13. "Giving Constructive Feedback," https://www.cabrillo.edu/services/jobs/pdfs/giving-feedback.pdf, accessed February 16, 2016.

14. van Ments, *The Effective Use of Role-Play*, 107–10.

15. Ibid.

16. Sivasailam Thiagarajan, "Instructional Games, Simulations, and Role-Plays," in *The ASTD Training and Development Handbook*, ed. Robert L. Craig (New York: McGraw-Hill, 1996), 526–28.

17. Ibid., 526.

18. Ibid., 527.

19. van Ments, *The Effective Use of Role-Play*, 145.

20. Thiagarajan, "Instructional Games, Simulations, and Role-Plays," 527.

21. Ibid.

22. Ibid.

23. Ibid.

24. Davis, *Tools for Teaching*, 113.

25. Alfred P. Rovai, "Facilitating Online Discussions Effectively," *Internet and Higher Education* 10, no. 1 (2007): 79, http://www.sciencedirect.com/science/article/pii/S1096751606000704.

26. Ibid., 81.

27. Davis, *Tools for Teaching*, 115.

28. Ibid., 113.

29. Rovai, "Facilitating Online Discussions Effectively," 81.

30. Ibid., 80.

31. Davis, *Tools for Teaching*, 114–15.

32. Rovai, "Facilitating Online Discussions Effectively," 83.

33. Tisha Bender, "Role Playing in Online Education: A Teaching Tool to Enhance Student Engagement and Sustained Learning," *Innovate: Journal of Online Education* 1, no. 5 (2005): Article 5, http://nsuworks.nova.edu/innovate/vol1/iss4/5.

34. Alexandra Ludewig and Iris Ludewig-Rohwer, "Does Web-Based Role-Play Establish a High Quality Learning Environment? Design versus Evaluation," *Issues in Educational Research* 23, no. 2 (2013): 164–78, http://www.iier.org.au/iier23/ludewig.pdf.

35. Richard E. Mayer, Andrew Stull, Krista DeLeeuw, Kevin Almeroth, Bruce Bimber, Dorothy Chun, Monica Bulger, Julie Campbell, Allan Knight, and Hangjin Zhang, "Clickers in College Classrooms: Fostering Learning with Questioning Methods in Large Lecture Classrooms," *Contemporary Educational Psychology* 34, no. 1 (2009): 51, http://www.sciencedirect.com/science/article/pii/S0361476X08000295; Svinicki and McKeachie, *McKeachie's Teaching Tips*, 271.

36. Davis, *Tools for Teaching*, 170.

37. Michael E. Lantz, "The Use of 'Clickers' in the Classroom: Teaching Innovation or Merely an Amusing Novelty?," *Computers in Human Behavior* 26, no. 4 (2010): 557, http://www.sciencedirect.com/science/article/pii/S0747563210000397.

38. Svinicki and McKeachie, McKeachie's *Teaching Tips*, 48.

39. Ibid.

40. Alden and Kirkhorn, "Case Studies," 507.

41. Ibid.

42. Svinicki and McKeachie, McKeachie's *Teaching Tips*, 178.

III

ASSESSING THE EFFECTIVENESS OF YOUR PLAGIARISM AND ETHICS AWARENESS TRAINING PROGRAM

As asserted by J. P. Huller of the Hobart Corporation, from a business perspective, all managers want to be "accepted, trusted, respected, and needed."[1] As providers of training in a complex academic environment, we similarly seek this credibility from a broad range of stakeholders. According to the 2014 industry report by *Training* magazine, 28 percent of respondents in the education industry reported a decrease in their training budgets over the previous year.[2] If we are to continue to provide plagiarism instruction within an educational environment, we must demonstrate to budget decision makers that investments to support this training yield valuable outcomes.

Fundamentally, the effectiveness of the training we provide depends on whether the training has achieved the objectives for which it has been designed. In the current training context, we consider whether our training has led to decreased incidents of plagiarism among students. However, this can be a complex and time-consuming objective to evaluate. What criteria should we use to assess training effectiveness? Should we assess student reactions to training, student knowledge after training, changes in student behavior, or academic code violations across the institution over time? Should we assess some combination of all of these factors?

In chapters 6 and 7, we examine multiple approaches to training assessment. Drawing on Kirkpatrick's four-level model of training evaluation,[3] we consider several strategies that trainers can take within each of these approaches to achieve multiple outcomes. In chapter 6, we examine how to assess the impact of the Plagiarism and Ethics Awareness Training (PEAT) program by measuring the affective responses that students have to the training content and process as well as the knowledge that students gain as a result of the training. In chapter 7, we analyze the impact of the PEAT program by determining the impact of training on student behavior as well as other key organizational-level outcomes. Finally, in chapter 8, we present strategies,

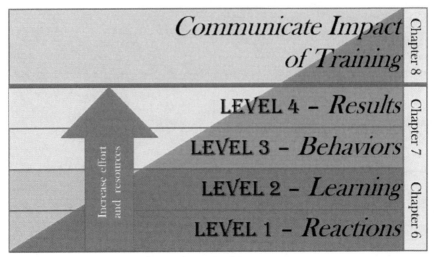

Increase effort and resources

Communicate Impact of Training — Chapter 8

LEVEL 4 – *Results* — Chapter 7

LEVEL 3 – *Behaviors*

LEVEL 2 – *Learning* — Chapter 6

LEVEL 1 – *Reactions*

Figure P3.1.   Components of Program Evaluation

guidelines, and suggestions for how to articulate the impact of your training program to key stakeholder groups.

Although the emphasis of this book is to present plagiarism as an ethical issue to trainees, it is important to acknowledge that to evaluate the effectiveness of this training, we must assess plagiarism knowledge and skills among trainees in addition to their *attitudes* toward plagiarism as an ethical issue. Therefore, this part of the book presents a full assessment model to evaluate trainee reactions to plagiarism prevention instruction, trainee learning (knowledge, skills, and attitudes), trainee behaviors, and organizational results. Without a full assessment of the plagiarism prevention instruction program, we cannot determine which components of our instruction are effective and which need to be improved. Ultimately, this part of the book provides you with resources to identify areas where training can be improved, to determine whether this training should continue, and to make a clear case to multiple stakeholders that this training is valuable.

NOTES

1. Donald L. Kirkpatrick, *Evaluating Training Programs: The Four Levels* (San Francisco: Berrett-Koehler, 1998), 13.

2. "2014 Training Industry Report," *Training*, November/December 2014, 21, https://trainingmag.com/trgmag-article/2014-training-industry-report.

3. Kirkpatrick, *Evaluating Training Programs*, 15.

6

Did They Like It? Did They Learn?

Assessing Student Reactions and Knowledge

The evaluation of trainee reactions centers on the assessment of participant perceptions, emotions, and individual appraisals of the training experience.[1] Kirkpatrick characterizes these reactions as a measure of customer satisfaction and emphasizes the importance of eliciting not simply any reaction from training participants but a positive reaction in particular.[2] The evaluation of trainee reactions is frequently derided not due to their lack of importance but because they tend to be the only type of training outcome that is evaluated.[3] Alliger and colleagues[4] suggest that trainee reactions can provide more valuable feedback to trainers if they are divided into two categories: affective reactions and utility judgments. Affective reactions represent the general feeling that trainees form about the training, whereas utility judgments reflect the beliefs that trainees develop regarding the usefulness of the training.

The future of your Plagiarism and Ethics Awareness Training (PEAT) program depends on positive trainee reactions for two primary reasons: learner motivation and word of mouth.[5] If participants do not respond favorably to your plagiarism instruction, they are not likely to be *motivated to learn*. Although positive trainee reactions do not guarantee that learning will take place, negative reactions almost always decrease the likelihood that participants will learn in your training sessions. Trainee reactions also impact word of mouth in that participants with positive reactions will speak more highly of the training experience to budget decision makers, potential future participants, and other instructors. This will improve the likelihood of your program's survival.

IMPORTANCE AND LIMITATIONS OF TRAINEE REACTIONS

Kirkpatrick[6] suggests that it is important to measure trainee reactions for several reasons. First, reactions give us feedback that can support the evaluation of our instruction intervention. Furthermore, the comments provided by training participants can help us improve future training interventions. Additionally, the collection of trainee reactions can signal to participants that the trainers care about doing a good job and sincerely want to be effective in facilitating positive training outcomes among participants. If we do not collect trainee reactions, we send the message that we know what is best for participants and do not need to hear from them to know how well we have done. This can exacerbate negative trainee reactions to our intervention. Finally, trainee reactions provide data that can be quantitatively summarized and used to create performance standards for future programs. It is important to recognize that *trainee reactions typically will not signify how much trainees have learned.*[7] However, by collecting trainee reactions, we give participants the chance to *reveal how they felt about learning* in the program.[8]

MEASURING TRAINEE REACTIONS

Measuring trainee reactions is important and fairly easy to do.[9] The most common method of collecting trainee reactions is through a *reaction* form. These forms can vary in their design, content, administration, and effectiveness. Kirkpatrick[10] offers these guidelines to keep in mind when designing your reaction form:

1. Identify the areas in which you desire feedback from the participants.
2. Design the form to collect trainee reactions in a numerical format (i.e., use a survey with a Likert scale to convert satisfaction with training to values ranging from 1 to 5).
3. Allow for and encourage written comments and suggestions from trainees.
4. Collect trainee reactions immediately following the conclusion of the training program.
5. Allow for anonymous responses to encourage candor and honesty from participants.

Several categories should factor into the design of a reaction questionnaire in order to assess the affective reactions and utility judgments that trainees have in response to your plagiarism instruction. Blanchard and Thacker[11] outline four considerations that can clarify trainee reactions to a training program: training relevance, training content and activities, trainer behavior, and training setting. By integrating these considerations into your trainee reaction questionnaire, you potentially gain important information that can help you make your plagiarism instruction more relevant to future participants, help you and other instruction providers be aware of training strengths and weaknesses, and provide training in settings that are more favorable for learning to take place:

- Training relevance: When you ask trainees if they found the training to be relevant or useful, you ascertain the perceived value of the training program (e.g., "Overall, how effective was the PEAT program in helping to increase your awareness of plagiarism as an ethical issue?"). When participants do not perceive value in a training program, they will lack interest, and through word of mouth, it can damage the training program's image and limit the attractiveness and effectiveness of this program to future potential participants. By assessing perceptions of training value, you can take action to change the beliefs of program participants or modify the training program itself.[12]

- Training content and activities: In addition to the overall training experience, you should assess all instructional tools and activities that you used during the training program. For example, if you had students break into small groups to discuss an ethics-based plagiarism scenario, you could ask the following question: "How helpful was it to work in small groups to analyze plagiarism as an ethical issue?" By collecting trainee assessments of this content, you can determine what materials and exercises were useful to participants. With this information, you can modify training to increase its relevance to participants and increase positive perceptions of the training overall.[13]

- Trainer behavior: Another useful reaction to collect is the responses that trainees have to the individual or individuals who provide the training. Care should be taken when constructing these questions. It is best to avoid general statements that elicit feedback about how friendly or entertaining participants find training providers to be (e.g., "The instructor was friendly and made the content of the PEAT program interesting."). While this is useful, it does not provide information about how *effective* the trainers are. A series of specific statements to assess the trainer's instruction behavior will better reveal the aggregate performance of the training provider: (1) the instructor effectively conveyed his or her knowledge of the ethical implications stemming from plagiarism, and (2) the instructor was able to explain ethical theories in a way that one could understand.[14]

- Training setting: A final area to assess when collecting training reactions relates to the facilities in which the training was provided. Include open-ended questions to determine if any aspects of the training setting interfered with the training process (e.g., "Was the classroom setup conducive for the PEAT activities and content?"). This information is valuable if you are planning to continue the training program and use the same setting to provide training to future participants.[15]

In many instances, a typical course assessment form will not always include these four components. To remedy this, you may want to supplement your institutional assessment form with a trainee reaction questionnaire that incorporates the elements discussed above (see text box 6.1). If conducting an intracurricular (single session) PEAT session, then this would most certainly be warranted, as institutional assessment forms do not typically exist for these one-shot instruction sessions.

Text Box 6.1   Sample Trainee Reaction Questions

Training Relevance

How would you rate the overall effectiveness of the PEAT program? (1 = extremely ineffective, 10 = extremely effective)

Overall, how effective was the PEAT program in helping to increase your awareness of plagiarism as an ethical issue? (1 = extremely ineffective, 10 = extremely effective)

Did the PEAT program meet your expectations? (1 = not at all, 10 = very much)

How would you rate the overall importance of the PEAT program? (1 = extremely unimportant, 10 = extremely important)

Would you recommend the PEAT program to others? (1 = no, 10 = yes)

Training Content and Activities

How helpful were the following methods in conveying information about plagiarism as an ethical issue: assigned readings, PowerPoint slides, instructor lecture, role plays, case studies, small-group discussions, and full-class discussions? (1 = extremely ineffective, 10 = extremely effective)

Rank the following PEAT program activities from least important to most important: assigned readings, PowerPoint slides, instructor lecture, role plays, case studies, small-group discussions, full-class discussions. (rank-order question)

The amount of content presented in the PEAT program was appropriate for the time allotted to these sessions. (1 = strongly disagree, 10 = strongly agree)

What activities should be added to improve your learning experience in the PEAT program? (open-ended question)

What activities should be omitted to improve your learning experience in the PEAT program? (open-ended question)

Trainer Behavior

Please rate the instructor's communication skills. (1 = very poor, 10 = very strong)

The instructor effectively conveyed his or her knowledge of the ethical implications stemming from plagiarism. (1 = strongly disagree, 10 = strongly agree)

The instructor appeared to be interested in the plagiarism and ethical issues. (1 = strongly disagree, 10 = strongly agree)

The trainer clearly communicated the purpose of this training. (1 = strongly disagree, 10 = strongly agree)

The trainer was considerate toward participants. (1 = strongly disagree, 10 = strongly agree)

The trainer encouraged questions from participants. (1 = strongly disagree, 10 = strongly agree)

The instructor was able to explain ethical theories in a way that I could understand. (1 = strongly disagree, 10 = strongly agree)

Training Setting

Was the classroom setup conducive for the PEAT content and activities? (1 = not at all conducive, 10 = extremely conducive)

Was the technology used in the PEAT program effective? (1 = very ineffective, 10 = very effective)

How could the classroom setup be improved for future PEAT sessions? (open-ended question)

Note: Questions adapted from P. Nick Blanchard and James W. Thacker, *Effective Training: Systems, Strategies, and Practices* (Upper Saddle River, NJ: Prentice Hall, 1999), 233, and Kenneth N. Wexley and Gary P. Latham, *Developing and Training Human Resources in Organizations* (Upper Saddle River, NJ: Prentice Hall, 2002), 129–30, 134.

ASSESSMENT OF TRAINEE LEARNING GAINED FROM PEAT

It is entirely possible that participants leave a training session with very favorable reactions but minimal if any knowledge gained from the training. Although we have established the importance of favorable training reactions and the measurement thereof, it does not preclude the measurement of trainee learning. Kirkpatrick asserts that "learning can be defined as the extent to which participants change attitudes, improve knowledge, and/or increase skill as a result of attending the program."[16] The PEAT program is designed to modify students' attitudes regarding the ethicality of plagiarism. Your training objectives feed directly into this assessment of what trainees learned from participating in your training program. As we discussed in the introduction to part III, the knowledge and skills that we assess as part of trainee learning will relate primarily to a traditional plagiarism instruction approach focusing on what plagiarism is and how to avoid it. As the emphasis of this book is to present plagiarism as an ethical issue, it is critical to also assess any change in trainee attitudes toward plagiarism and the ethics of plagiarism *in addition to* assessing the practical knowledge and skills gained from this instruction. We discuss each component of learning below: attitudes, knowledge, and skills.

The first area in which we can assess learning is in participant *attitudes*. Attitudes are "evaluative statements" that reflect our feelings toward "objects, people, or events."[17] They are most frequently assessed by attitude scales administered in a survey. For plagiarism instruction, we may be interested in assessing the change in participant attitudes toward plagiarism as an ethical issue. As we discuss below, it can be difficult to measure changes in attitude for a variety of reasons, but some established scales exist that can help you in this regard.

Most often, training focuses on improving declarative *knowledge*, or factual knowledge, that is commonly measured by a paper-and-pencil type of exam immediately on the conclusion of training. Alliger and colleagues[18] further break down knowledge into two categories: knowledge measured immediately following training (declarative knowledge) and knowledge measured at a later time (knowledge retention). Thus, in the case of plagiarism instruction, we would look for participants to be able to identify key content and be able to retain it for some period of time after receiving instruction with emphasis on pragmatic knowledge about what plagiarism is and how one can avoid it.

Blanchard and Thacker[19] take a different approach to classifying knowledge. They too start with declarative knowledge, but they discuss two additional categories of higher-level knowledge: *procedural knowledge* and *strategic knowledge*. Procedural knowledge represents how participants organize what they learn into knowledge structures. Strategic knowledge is when participants are able to use knowledge gained from training in solving problems. Both procedural and strategic knowledge are higher levels of knowledge learning than is declarative knowledge. Given the nature of plagiarism instruction, we want participants to exhibit knowledge-learning outcomes beyond declarative knowledge so that they are able to employ techniques to avoid plagiarism throughout their academic and professional careers.

Sometimes, training presents content where learning is best assessed as a *skill*. Alliger and colleagues[20] refer to this as *skill demonstration*, or the demonstration of trained behavior immediately following training. Blanchard and Thacker[21] further delineate skill into two levels: *compilation* and *automaticity*. When you complete skills at a compilation level, you are able to thoughtfully reproduce the skill. When you are able to complete the skill quickly and without much thought, you have achieved the skill level of automaticity. Let's assume in the case of plagiarism instruction that we want participants to gain skills in research and writing. More often than not, we would assess these skills at the compilation level immediately following training with the hope that these skills become more automatic as students continue to practice them throughout their academic careers.

IMPORTANCE AND LIMITATIONS OF TRAINEE LEARNING

Mathieu, Tannenbaum, and Salas[22] found that trainee learning moderately correlates with immediate job behaviors. From this, we can conclude that higher levels of student learning during plagiarism instruction sessions will lead to some improvement in student plagiarism behavior immediately following this instruction. However, typically, our assessment of skills learned will immediately follow training. Therefore, we cannot assume that participants will transfer what they have learned to their work contexts (or, in the case of plagiarism instruction in an academic context, their *class* work contexts).

How to Measure Trainee Knowledge

The most common method of assessing learning is to examine *declarative knowledge* with paper-and-pencil tests prior to the training and compare it with results collected during or immediately following the training program.[23] If possible, these pre- and posttest scores can be compared with the pre- and posttest scores of a group who did not receive the training (a control group) to demonstrate that any improvement in score occurred due to the training provided and not some other factor (e.g., familiarity with the testing instrument). Figure 6.1 illustrates how to employ pre- and posttests in your assessment of training knowledge.

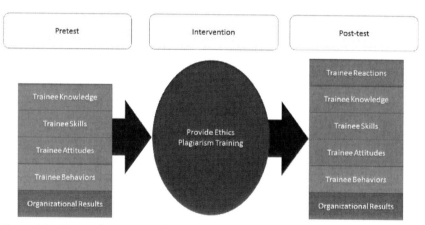

Figure 6.1.   Pre- and Posttest Design to Assess Trainee Knowledge

There are many advantages to using paper-and-pencil tests to assess learning among training participants. They are easy to proctor and record, they can cover a large and broad array of content, and they have the potential to yield accurate and consistent measures of knowledge gained among participants.[24] Some disadvantages of these tests of learning are that they may be contaminated by test anxiety in participants. Further, it can be challenging to develop good test questions. Blanchard and Thacker[25] identify seven steps to developing quality multiple-choice questions to evaluate learning:

1. Review your training goals to focus and refresh your understanding of the content areas that you seek to assess.
2. Use clear and simple writing when constructing your questions. Be concise.

3. When choosing alternatives to the correct answer, draw on the common mistakes that participants make during training. Make the alternative answers plausible and realistic.
4. Avoid regularly making the incorrect responses shorter than the correct response.
5. Typically, four response choices are sufficient. More than four responses take longer to read, and it is amply difficult to write three reasonable choices that are incorrect.
6. To pretest your questions, give the test to individuals who know the training material. Solicit feedback on clarity and take note of all questions that they answer incorrectly. Make revisions in light of the pretest feedback and performance.
7. Retest your revised questions by giving the test to two groups of students: an experienced group and an inexperienced group. You should see that the experienced group performs at a much higher level than the inexperienced group.

Multiple-choice tests are an appropriate assessment tool, assuming that the training content that you want to evaluate falls in the areas of declarative knowledge, knowledge retention (where you would administer the test some period of time after training is completed), procedural knowledge (where participants would answer questions to demonstrate knowledge about process), and strategic knowledge (where participants would answer questions that show they can use training knowledge to solve problems). In text box 6.2, we provide sample paper-and-pencil questions that assess trainee learning based on the stakeholder model and the Giving Voice to Values framework presented in chapter 4.

Multiple-choice questions may also be appropriate to assess a change in trainee *attitudes*—though we would advise that you consult the academic literature to locate a valid scale to assess the trainee attitudes. Because the purpose of this book is to present plagiarism instruction as an ethical issue, it is critical to examine any changes that may occur in participant attitudes as a result of plagiarism instruction. One potential method to assess these attitudes is the Multidimensional Ethics Scale,[26] which was developed based on a three-dimensional theoretical conceptualization of ethical judgment. The development and refinement of this scale included tests of multiple versions across multiple samples ranging from students to business practitioners. The results from these iterations yielded the final three-dimensional, eight-item ethics scale. These scaled items should be presented with a plagiarism scenario to elicit ethical judgments toward plagiarism, as presented in text box 6.3.

Another method to assess trainee attitudes toward plagiarism is the Theory of Planned Behavior.[27] This model has been employed in research to examine ethical behavior as well as academic misconduct.[28] The Theory of Planned Behavior asserts that three factors determine whether an individual will plan to commit a particular behavior (behavioral intentions) and that an individual's behavioral intentions will predict his or her consequent implementation of that behavior. Behavioral intentions

Text Box 6.2   Sample Paper-and-Pencil Assessment Questions for
Stakeholder Analysis and Giving Voice to Values

Stakeholder Analysis
- In the PEAT program, we discussed five sample stakeholders who are impacted by Jane when she chooses to plagiarize. Name three stakeholders and explain how they are impacted by Jane's action.
- Identify all stakeholders impacted in the following plagiarism scenario:

   > Susan finds a flash drive in a computer at the library. While trying to identify the owner, she notices that the owner took the same biology course that she is currently taking. The course is assignment intensive with many labs and short papers. She has a lab report due this week, and this has been particularly challenging and is about 50 percent completed. When she looks at the report the owner wrote for this particular lab, she thinks it is much better. Knowing that it would take her another two hours to complete her own lab report, she decides to submit the report that she found on the flash drive.

- One stakeholder group that is impacted by Jane's plagiarism is her future employers. Explain why and how her future employers are impacted by Jane's action.

Giving Voice to Values
- According to Giving Voice to Values, what response can you provide to the following rationalization: *plagiarism is standard practice at this school?*
- According to Giving Voice to Values, what response can you provide to the following rationalization: *plagiarism is a victimless crime?*
- According to Giving Voice to Values, what response can you provide to the following rationalization: *if the professor wrote better assignments, we wouldn't be able to plagiarize?*

are determined by "(a) attitudes toward the behavior, that is, beliefs about a specific behavior and its consequences; (b) subjective norms, that is, normative expectations of other people who are important to the actor regarding the behavior; and (c) perceived behavioral control, that is, the perceived difficulty or ease of performing the behavior."[29] In table 6.1, we present a measure of the Theory of Planned Behavior from the work of Stone and colleagues[30] with some items adapted to apply specifically to plagiarism. Items 1 through 7 measure *attitudes* toward plagiarism. However, it may be useful to include the full measure in your pre- and posttraining assessment

Text Box 6.3   Assessing Student Attitudes Using the Multidimensional Ethics Scale[1]

Desmond's teacher assigned a business paper six weeks before it was due. Five weeks pass, and Desmond has been busy with work from other classes. He also works after school, making it difficult to get started on the paper. He wants to do well since the paper counts for 20 percent of the course grade. If Desmond fails the class, he could lose his scholarship, which would prevent him from returning to school the following semester.

Desmond soon feels panicky because the paper requires more than one week of effort. His solution is to photocopy pages from sources that deal with his topic. Using whole paragraphs from these pages, he hurriedly puts together his paper. He completes the assignment, including a reference list with the sources he used.

Indicate your level of agreement with the statements below. (1 = strongly disagree, 10 = strongly agree)
*The action Desmond took was fair.
Desmond's action is culturally acceptable.
Desmond's action violates an "unspoken promise."
Desmond was not morally right.
Desmond's action is traditionally unacceptable.
*Desmond did not violate an unwritten contract.
Desmond's action was unjust.
Desmond's behavior would be unacceptable to my family.

---

[1] R. Eric Reidenbach and Donald P. Robin, "Toward the Development of a Multidimensional Scale for Improving Evaluations of Business Ethics," *Journal of Business Ethics* 9, no. 8 (1990): 639–53, http://www.jstor.org/stable/25072080.

*Statements are reverse coded.

to get a more complete picture of students' perceptions of plagiarism and its context in that academic environment.

We offer a word of caution when assessing attitudes, as it is a difficult task for a variety of reasons. First, attitudes are difficult to observe. We rely on participants honestly reporting their perceptions when responding to these scales. Furthermore, social desirability bias may cause participants to answer in a way that does not reflect their true attitudes. In the case of plagiarism and the ethics of plagiarism, participants may perceive that it is more socially desirable to display negative attitudes toward plagiarism. These challenges may add to the difficulty of the assessment of attitudes in particular when using paper-and-pencil tests.

Table 6.1. Theory of Planned Behavior Scale to Assess Student Attitudes toward Plagiarism

Key Variable	Statements
Attitude toward plagiarism These items are measured with a response scale ranging from strongly disagree to strongly agree.	• It is important to report observations of plagiarism by other students. (reverse scored) • It is always wrong to plagiarize. (reverse scored) • I would report an incidence of plagiarism by a student whom I do not know. (reverse scored) • I would report an incidence of plagiarism by a student whom I consider a friend. (reverse scored) • Reporting incidences of plagiarism is necessary to be fair to honest students. (reverse scored) • Students should go ahead and plagiarize if they know they can get away with it. • I would let another student plagiarize from my paper if he or she asked.
Subjective norm Typically, these items are measured with frequency-type response choices.	• Approximately what percentage of students do you think engage in plagiarism? • In the past year, how often, if ever, have you suspected that another student plagiarized an assignment? • Some of my friends plagiarize and have not been caught. • How frequently do you think plagiarism has occurred in classes at your school?
Perceived behavioral control These items are measured with a response scale ranging from strongly disagree to strongly agree.	• If I wanted to plagiarize my work, it would be easy. • In my classes, it would be fairly easy for me to plagiarize. • It is difficult for me to plagiarize and not get caught. (reverse scored)
Intention These items are measured with a response scale ranging from very unlikely to very likely.	• How likely are you to consider turning in another's work done as one's own? • How likely are you to consider writing a paper for another student? • How likely are you to consider plagiarizing a paper in any way using the Internet as a source? • How likely are you to consider using unapproved materials to complete an assignment?
Behavior These items are measured with a response scale ranging from never to many times.	• If or how often during college have you copied a few sentences from a published or Internet source but not given credit to the author? • If or how often during college have you copied from another student and turned it in as your own work? • If or how often during college have you turned in work done by someone else?

If your training goals center on the attainment of *skills* or behavior, you will likely find that multiple-choice or paper-and-pencil tests are not sufficient. While paper-and-pencil tests may indicate that the trainee understands a skill or process, they do not illustrate if a trainee can actually demonstrate that skill.[31]

Some methods for assessing the attainment of skills include simulations, role plays, behavioral reproduction, case studies, and ratings of training performance.[32] Gordon and Isenberg[33] found that the rating of training performance can be highly dependent on the raters—more so than the trainee and his or her performance. They recommend the use of multiple raters to prevent this problem. This involves time, expense, and the coordination of the raters to address any variations in their assessments. It also requires the construction of a performance test evaluation form.

When assessing skill demonstration after plagiarism instruction, you might consider the type of skill you want trainees to demonstrate in addition to your available time and resources. A case study may be sufficient for you to assess trainee skill. Another alternative may be a pencil-and-paper performance test, as shown in figure 6.2.

TURNITIN.COM COMMON CONTENT SKILLS TEST

Instructions: Identify each of the numbered items in the figure below.

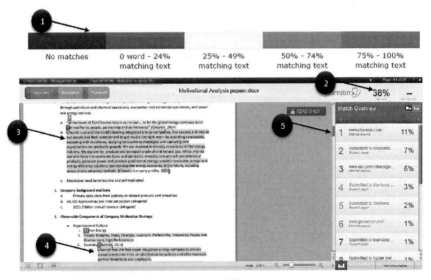

Figure 6.2. Turnitin.com Common Content Skills Test

Answer Key:

1. Similarity index scale.
2. Paper similarity index score.
3. Verbatim text attributed to a resource but not indicated as a direct quote.
4. Verbatim text not attributed to a resource and not indicated as a direct quote.
5. Lists of sources from all common content matches found in student document.

Ultimately, you want your chosen assessment of skill to match the actual tasks of the behaviors you hope students will perform in their academic work contexts. One possible method of skills assessment is to assign a research writing task at the conclusion of training that requires trainees to draw research from a specific set of resources and submit their finished assignments to some type of plagiarism software. Through this performance test, you can assess trainee skill at avoiding plagiarism. When combined with additional assessments of knowledge and of attitude, you will achieve a complete evaluation of trainee learning.

NOTES

1. P. Nick Blanchard and James W. Thacker, *Effective Training: Systems, Strategies, and Practices* (Upper Saddle River, NJ: Prentice Hall, 1964), 225.

2. Donald L. Kirkpatrick, *Evaluating Training Programs: The Four Levels* (San Francisco: Berrett-Koehler, 1998), 22.

3. Blanchard and Thacker, *Effective Training*, 23; Lise M. Saari, Terry R. Johnson, Stephen D. McLaughlin, and Denise M. Zimmerlie, "A Survey of Management and Education Practices in U.S. Companies," *Personnel Psychology* 41, no. 4 (1988): 739, doi:10.1111/j.1744-6570.1988.tb00650.x; George B. Yancey and Lynne Kelly, "The Inappropriateness of Using Participants' Reactions to Evaluate Effectiveness of Training," *Psychological Reports* 66, no. 3 (1990): 937–38, http://www.amsciepub.com/doi/pdf/10.2466/pr0.1990.66.3.937; Kenneth N. Wexley and Gary A. Yukl, *Organizational Behavior and Industrial Psychology: Readings with Commentary* (New York: Oxford University Press, 1975), 555–60.

4. Tannenbaum Alliger, Trayer Bennett, and Allison Shotland, "Meta-Analysis of the Relationship among Training Criteria," *Personnel Psychology* 50, no. 2 (1997): 344, http://onlinelibrary.wiley.com/doi/10.1111/j.1744-6570.1997.tb00911.x/abstract.

5. Kirkpatrick, *Evaluating Training Programs*, 27–41.

6. Ibid., 25.

7. Alliger et al., "Meta-Analysis of the Relationship among Training Criteria," 344.

8. Blanchard and Thacker, *Effective Training*, 230.

9. Kirkpatrick, *Evaluating Training Programs*, 25.

10. Ibid., 26.

11. Blanchard and Thacker, *Effective Training*, 230–32.

12. Ibid., 230.

13. Ibid., 230–32.

14. Ibid., 232.

15. Ibid.

16. Kirkpatrick, *Evaluating Training Programs*, 20.

17. Stephen P. Robbins, *Organizational Behavior: Concepts and Self-Assessment* (Upper Saddle River, NJ: Prentice Hall College Division, 1998), chapter 3.

18. Alliger et al., "Meta-Analysis of the Relationship among Training Criteria," 345.

19. Blanchard and Thacker, *Effective Training*, 235.

20. Alliger et al., "Meta-Analysis of the Relationship among Training Criteria," 345.

21. Blanchard and Thacker, *Effective Training*, 238.

22. John E. Mathieu, Scott I. Tannenbaum, and Eduardo Salas, "Influences of Individual and Situational Characteristics on Measures of Training Effectiveness," *Academy of Management Journal* 35, no. 4 (1992): 841–42, http://www.jstor.org/stable/256317.

23. Kenneth N. Wexley and Gary P. Latham, *Developing and Training Human Resources in Organizations* (Upper Saddle River, NJ: Prentice Hall, 2002), 137–40.

24. Blanchard and Thacker, *Effective Training*, 160.

25. Ibid., 236.

26. R. Eric Reidenbach and Donald P. Robin, "Some Initial Steps toward Improving the Measurement of Ethical Evaluations of Marketing Activities," *Journal of Business Ethics* 7, no. 11 (1988): 871–79, http://www.jstor.org/stable/25071847; R. Eric Reidenbach and Donald P. Robin, "Toward the Development of a Multidimensional Scale for Improving Evaluations of Business Ethics," *Journal of Business Ethics* 9, no. 8 (1990): 639–53, http://www.jstor.org/stable/25072080.

27. Ajzen Icek, "From Intentions to Actions: A Theory of Planned Behavior," in *Action-Control: From Cognition to Behavior*, ed. Julius Kuhl and Jurgen Beckmann (New York: Springer-Verlag, 1985), 11–39; Icek Ajzen, "The Theory of Planned Behavior," *Organizational Behavior and Human Decision Processes* 50, no. 2 (1991): 179–211, http://www.sciencedirect.com/science/article/pii/074959789190020T.

28. Man Kit Chang, "Predicting Unethical Behavior: A Comparison of the Theory of Reasoned Action and the Theory of Planned Behavior," *Journal of Business Ethics* 17, no. 16 (1998): 1825–34, http://link.springer.com/article/10.1023%2FA%3A1005721401993; Thomas H. Stone, I. M. Jawahr, and Jennifer L. Kisamore, "Predicting Academic Misconduct Intentions and Behavior Using the Theory of Planned Behavior and Personality," *Basic and Applied Social Psychology* 32, no. 1 (2010): 35–45, http://www.tandfonline.com/doi/pdf/10.1080/01973530903539895.

29. Stone et al., "Predicting Academic Misconduct Intentions and Behavior Using the Theory of Planned Behavior and Personality," 36.

30. Ibid., 45.

31. M. Fein, "Item Writing and Scoring," in *ASTD's Best on Measuring and Evaluating Learning*, vol. 2 (Danvers, MA: American Society for Training and Development Press, 2013), 96–97.

32. Alliger et al., "Meta-Analysis of the Relationship among Training Criteria," 346; Wexley and Latham, *Developing and Training Human Resources in Organizations*, 137–40.

33. Michael E. Gordon and John F. Isenberg, "Validation of an Experimental Training Criterion for Machinists," *Journal of Industrial Teacher Education* 12, no. 2 (1975): 72–78.

7

Did the Training Make a Difference?

Assessing Student Behavior and Organizational Results

Although trainees may have gained knowledge and skills as a result of the Plagiarism and Ethics Awareness Training (PEAT) program and accompanying plagiarism prevention instruction, this does not guarantee that the knowledge or skills gained from training will transfer into behavior. The aim of Kirkpatrick's third level of training evaluation is to determine what change in behavior has occurred as a result of participating in the training.[1] For the purposes of this discussion, many of the behavioral examples used will relate more directly to traditional plagiarism prevention instruction which emphasizes teaching students how not to plagiarize rather than the PEAT program which focuses on altering students' attitudes about why plagiarism is unethical. As we articulate in chapter 1, these two training programs go hand in hand.

Kirkpatrick points out that this level of evaluation poses more challenges than assessing training reactions and learning for several reasons. First, trainees need the *opportunity* to change their behavior. Thus, in the case of plagiarism instruction in a college setting, trainees cannot apply the knowledge and skills they've learned about plagiarism until they receive a writing or research assignment. Second, even when trainees have an opportunity to change their behavior, they may not do so immediately. It is difficult to predict *when* trainees will change their behavior. Finally, when trainees *do* change their behavior, the types of intrinsic and extrinsic rewards they receive will determine whether this change is temporary or longer lasting. For trainees who use knowledge and skills from plagiarism instruction, they may receive intrinsic rewards through the experience of satisfaction and pride as they integrate these new skills into their study behavior. Or these trainees may receive extrinsic rewards, such as higher marks on their writing assignments or praise from their instructors. These rewards will reinforce the posttraining behavioral changes of trainees and increase the likelihood that these changes will continue into the future.[2]

As discussed in chapter 6, it is best to assess reactions and learning immediately after training. However, the challenges discussed above suggest that timing is an important consideration when planning the assessment of behavioral changes. Thus, when assessing changes in behavior, we must consider not only *how* to evaluate but also *when* and *how often* to evaluate.[3]

HOW TO MEASURE TRAINEE BEHAVIOR

Kirkpatrick[4] suggests seven guidelines to shape evaluations of behavioral change: use a control group, allow time for change to occur, evaluate before and after training, collect evaluation data from individuals who know the behavior, get a 100 percent response rate, repeat evaluations to gauge change into the future, and weigh the costs versus the benefits of the evaluation. We discuss each of these in the following paragraphs.

If possible, utilize a control group. As discussed in chapter 6, control groups refer to groups that do not receive training. By comparing the behavior of the control group against the group that received training (the *treatment*, or *experimental*, *group*), you can make the argument that behavioral improvements exhibited by the experimental group are indicative of training success.[5] However, it is important to ensure that the control and treatment groups are equal on all factors that may impact the behavior you are evaluating. In the case of plagiarism instruction, you'd want members from the control and experimental groups to have similar skill levels and backgrounds in research and writing. For example, if your treatment group is comprised of freshmen who are enrolled in a 100-level composition class and received a C on their first high-stakes writing assignment, you want to draw your control group from the same population.

Before evaluation, allocate time to allow for behavior changes to occur. You want to give your trainees time to encounter an opportunity to implement new behavior, consider the behavior, and try it out. For trainees who receive plagiarism instruction, this may mean that you evaluate trainee behavior used in writing assignments during the semester in which training was provided as well as the following semester(s).

If pragmatic or possible, evaluate behavior before and after the training. If you are offering plagiarism instruction in an open workshop where preregistration is not required, evaluating behavior prior to training may not be possible. However, if you provide this instruction as part of a class or as a stand-alone class, you can assess the behavior of training participants prior to and following instruction by observing performance on writing assignments or examining trainee levels of unoriginal content in their assignments using a cloud service, such as Turnitin.

Collect survey or interview data from individuals who are knowledgeable about trainee behavior. This can include trainees, their tutors, their instructors or teaching assistants, writing center coaches, and administrators who monitor or are involved in academic misconduct. Kirkpatrick advises that we consider four questions when identifying individuals to collect this data from: "Who is best qualified? Who is most reliable? Who is most available? [and] Are there any reasons why one or more of the possible candidates should not be used?"[6]

Keeping these questions in mind for a PEAT program, while trainees are likely the best qualified to determine whether their plagiarism behaviors have changed, they may not be willing to admit that they used to plagiarize in the first place, compromising their reliability. Instructors, teaching assistants, and writing center coaches are qualified and more reliable but are less available, particularly as you seek to collect interview data from them. However, they may be more willing and able to provide survey responses.

While surveys are more practical to administer, response rates may suffer, and the data you collect using this tool typically lack the depth that you can gather with interviews. Yet interviews are time consuming and difficult to administer to a large number of people. It may be worth conducting patterned interviews with a small sample of trainees in combination with a survey of their writing instructors.

A training evaluator may use the following questions, adapted from Kirkpatrick,[7] to assess behavior that students acquire from the PEAT program:

- What specific activities were taught and promoted in the PEAT program?
- When you completed the PEAT program, how eager were you to modify your behavior when writing research assignments?
- How well prepared were you to implement the behavior suggested in the PEAT program?
- If you are not implementing the behavior taught and promoted in the PEAT program, why not? How significant are each of the following? (1 = not significant, 10 = very significant)
  a. This behavior isn't feasible in my situation.
  b. This behavior does not fit with the cultural norms of my situation.
  c. I haven't found the time to implement this behavior.
  d. I tried implementing this behavior, and it didn't work.
  e. Other reasons (ask trainee to specify these reasons).
- What is the likelihood that you will modify (continue to modify) your behavior in the future? (1 = very unlikely, 10 = extremely likely)
- How can we improve the PEAT program to make it more helpful to future participants?

If evaluators lack time to conduct individual interviews, a survey to assess the impact of the PEAT program on behavior could be used (see table 7.1). If practical, try for a 100 percent response rate but settle for a strategic sample. When you are evaluating behavioral change, "something beats nothing,"[8] so, though a 100 percent response rate is ideal, it may not be realistic or practical. Determine how much time and money you are willing to spend to collect these data. Then you may want to proceed by surveying or interviewing a random subset of trainees who represent average participants. Alternatively, you might consider evaluating trainees who seem

Table 7.1. Sample PEAT Program Behavior Assessment Survey

Instructions: The purpose of this survey is to assess the degree that PEAT program participants have applied principles and techniques that they learned to their academic assignments. The findings of this questionnaire will help us evaluate the effectiveness of the PEAT program and plagiarism prevention instruction training. This will also help us identify opportunities to make this training more helpful to future participants.

PEAT Program Skills

1. Considering the ethical implications of attributing ideas to their authors.	(1 = I do this less now than I did before the PEAT program, 10 = I do this more now than I did before the PEAT program)
2. Considering the ethical implications if I submit plagiarized work as my own.	(1 = I do this less now than I did before the PEAT program, 10 = I do this more now than I did before the PEAT program)
3. Consider the stakeholders impacted if I plagiarize an assignment.	(1 = I do this less now than I did before the PEAT program, 10 = I do this more now than I did before the PEAT program)
4. Consider how to counter my classmates' rationalizations for plagiarism.	(1 = I do this less now than I did before the PEAT program, 10 = I do this more now than I did before the PEAT program)
5. Reporting instances of plagiarism when I am aware of them.	(1 = I do this less now than I did before the PEAT program, 10 = I do this more now than I did before the PEAT program)

Plagiarism Prevention Training Skills

1. Documenting sources in my reference list.	(1 = I do this less now than I did before the PEAT program, 10 = I do this more now than I did before the PEAT program)
2. Documenting sources using in-line citations.	(1 = I do this less now than I did before the PEAT program, 10 = I do this more now than I did before the PEAT program)
3. Paraphrase sources when taking notes.	(1 = I do this less now than I did before the PEAT program, 10 = I do this more now than I did before the PEAT program)
4. Paraphrasing sources that I refer to when writing my assignments.	(1 = I do this less now than I did before the PEAT program, 10 = I do this more now than I did before the PEAT program)
5. Ensuring that I properly attribute ideas to their authors.	(1 = I do this less now than I did before the PEAT program, 10 = I do this more now than I did before the PEAT program)
6. Indicating directly quoted content as direct quotes.	(1 = I do this less now than I did before the PEAT program, 10 = I do this more now than I did before the PEAT program)

Assessment survey adapted from Donald L. Kirkpatrick, *Evaluating Training Programs: The Four Levels* (San Francisco: Berrett-Koehler, 1998), 62.

to be the *least likely* to change their behavior. The logic behind the latter sampling technique is that it provides a conservative assessment of behavioral change

Iterate evaluation at suitable times. As discussed previously, it is impossible to predict when or if a trainee's behavior will change and whether this change will endure over time. Therefore, we must determine the appropriate times to collect data following training. For example, the 2012 ACT National Curriculum Survey reported that instructors of first-year college courses in writing, English, social studies, and physics assign 3.48 to 5.1 papers (exceeding five pages) per semester. Trainees who tend to enroll in these subjects likely have an increased opportunity to change their behavior, and as a result we have more opportunity to evaluate these changes. On the other hand, according to the same survey, instructors of first-year college courses in mathematics, biology, chemistry, and earth sciences assign .72 to 1.62 papers (exceeding five pages) per semester. Trainees enrolled in these subjects may take longer to enact behavioral changes.

Assess the cost versus the benefits of evaluating behavior change. Most often, the cost of evaluating behavior stems from the considerable amount of staff time required to conduct these evaluations. Should you decide to bring external consultants into the organization to plan the evaluation program or implement specific evaluations, these costs also must be considered. At the same time, you should bear in mind the benefits stemming from evaluation that include changes in behavior. If these changes or training results lead to valuable benefits, it stands to reason that this warrants higher expenditures to design and conduct an evaluation of the program. In a 2011 survey of 1,055 college presidents, 55 percent indicated that they believe plagiarism has increased at their institutions.[9] A plagiarism instruction program at one of these 1,055 colleges will likely be perceived as providing a valuable benefit. However, investments in evaluating training are typically warranted for training programs that are offered on a recurring basis, as expenditures can be justified by potential improvements in future offerings.

SAMPLE TRAINEE BEHAVIOR MEASURES

We discussed and provided examples of two evaluation methods (patterned interview and survey) above. Here we review two additional methods to evaluate behavior change.

In chapter 6, we discussed using the Theory of Planned Behavior Scale to evaluate changes in trainee attitudes. This scale also can be used to assess changed behavior as it measures intentions to commit behavior. Research[10] has found the greatest predictor of behavior in individuals is their intention to commit that behavior. Furthermore, this questionnaire incorporates an assessment of skill by surveying trainees' perceived control of plagiarism behavior. This scale is presented as table 6.4 in chapter 6.[11]

Turnitin Overall Similarity Index scores highlight the common content in a student's electronic paper submissions. There are advantages and disadvantages to this technique. An advantage is that electronic submission of written assignments has dramatically increased in recent years. In a survey of over 1,000 higher education Turnitin customers, from 2004 to 2013, electronic submissions increased from approximately 500,000 to 45 million papers.[12] However, Turnitin.com as well as several researchers[13] caution us that Overall Similarity Index scores alone do not indicate that plagiarism has occurred in an assignment. For example, Bretag and Mahmud[14] point out that properly cited material may appear as common content in an electronic similarity report. Furthermore, conscientious students who submit drafts prior to a submission deadline may receive an Overall Similarity Index score of 100 percent on their final papers when they have not committed plagiarism. As such, these raw data may be misleading and should be used in combination with other evaluation methods.

KEY BARRIER OF TRAINING TRANSFER: HUMAN RESISTANCE TO CHANGE

The transition from learning in training programs to changing behavior outside of training poses a difficult challenge to the average trainee and an important consideration to the trainer. Kirkpatrick and Kirkpatrick suggest that most training programs "are effective to *the degree that they are properly implemented.*"[15] In other words, the success of your plagiarism instruction program can be determined by the extent to which trainees integrate what they've learned from this training into their day-to-day academic behavior. The term *transfer of training* tackles this challenge; it "refers to how much of what is learned in training transfers to the job [or relevant context of performance]."[16]

If Kirkpatrick and Kirkpatrick[17] are correct that most training programs would be effective if participants simply implemented what they learned from these programs, then why don't trainees follow through with what they've learned? A significant barrier to training transfer and overall training effectiveness is human resistance to change and lack of persistence in implementing change.[18] As humans, we default to what is comfortable and familiar even if we know that implementing changes will improve our lives in meaningful ways. Another issue is that the transfer of learning to behavior requires systematic and persistent effort on the part of the trainees. Careless note taking, stress, and poor time management have all been identified as common motivations of plagiarism.[19] Given that plagiarism instruction asks students to change their academic behavior and that these changes require disciplined and consistent effort, the transfer of training in this context poses a significant challenge. This is particularly difficult to sustain when trainees may not achieve desired results (high marks on writing assignments) in the short term.[20]

Facilitating Transfer of Training

Factors that can facilitate transfer of training can be categorized into three groups: conditions of practice, identical elements, and stimulus variability. Feedback, retention strategies, and goal setting also can support training transfers.[21] These factors should be considered when designing the training program. Some elements may not be practical given the specific context of the plagiarism instruction program you are implementing (e.g., stand-alone workshop vs. a semester-long course). We focus this discussion on factors that will facilitate the transfer of plagiarism instruction across a variety of formats to student behavior. For a more in-depth examination of training transfer strategies, see Blanchard and Thacker.[22]

Conditions of Practice

Conditions of practice integrate opportunities for trainees to practice skills within the training session. Research has shown that spaced practice, in which trainees practice for 30 minutes across eight separate days, is more effective than massed practice, in which trainees practice for 60 minutes across four separate days.[23] Although spaced practice can improve retention of knowledge and skills—a necessary prerequisite for training transfer to occur—it requires a longer training cycle. For more complex and difficult tasks, such as research and writing skills that may be included in plagiarism instruction, a combination of massed and spaced practice may be effective where a massed practice session is followed by several spaced practices over a period of time.[24]

An additional condition of practice involves whether trainees learn separate components of a task one at a time (part learning) or the whole task in one setting (whole learning).[25] This depends on whether the task can be reasonably divided into components as well as the complexity of the task. Thus, if the focus of your plagiarism instruction session is to discuss the definition of plagiarism and examples of plagiarism and to review citation techniques, it is plausible to use a whole learning approach in your training design. If you are also including research strategies and note-taking techniques, a part-learning approach may be more desirable. If your approach to plagiarism is more interdependent, you may consider using a third technique: *progressive part training*.[26] In a progressive part training approach, in session 1 you might focus on the definition and examples of plagiarism; in session 2, you'd review session 1 content and add research strategies; in session 3, you'd review sessions 1 and 2 content and add note-taking techniques; and in session 4, you review previous session content (from sessions 1 to 3) and add citation techniques.

A final condition of practice addresses the concept of *overlearning*. Overlearning is when trainees have successfully completed a task during training but continue with task practice as throughout the training sessions.[27] Overlearning improves retention of knowledge and skills,[28] which is particularly valuable for tasks that are not used as frequently,[29] as overlearning can lead to automaticity where appropriate research and citation techniques become reflexive among trainees in their academic environments.

Identical Elements

By including elements in plagiarism instruction that are identical to the academic work context that students will encounter after training, you increase the likelihood that trainees will transfer learning into behaviors. There are two areas in which you can seek to maximize similarity: task and environment.[30] For example, when providing plagiarism instruction to a group of engineering students, it is desirable to use examples that students will encounter in the engineering curriculum. If you are reviewing citation techniques for a group of psychology students, you should emphasize the American Psychological Association, as this is what psychology students will encounter for their written assignments as they advance in their curricula. On the topic of environment, if you are providing a research tutorial, you'd want to provide it, for example, in the appropriate library. Additionally, you may want to demonstrate how to access digital resources from off campus if most students tend to conduct their research from personal laptops at home.

Stimulus Variability

Because most writing assignments that students encounter in their academic careers are on distinct topics, it is impossible to produce fully identical elements in training practice. Because the performance situations will vary for students, you may want to provide them with a general framework so that trainees are better equipped to deal with the variety they encounter in their academic and professional careers.[31] For example, if you seek to teach students to critically analyze resources as part of your plagiarism prevention instruction, you may want to employ a framework on critically evaluating information. A sample framework is provided in text box 7.1. This framework instills in trainees general principles of evaluating resources that they can adapt and apply to a variety of courses and assignments that they may encounter in the future.

Additional Factors That Facilitate Training Transfer

Kirkpatrick and Kirkpatrick[32] suggest that resistance to change can be addressed by providing support and increasing accountability for behavioral change. Feedback, retention strategies, and goal setting may help in this endeavor. Providing trainees with feedback lets them know whether they need to adjust their behavior, can be encouraging and motivating, and can lead to performance improvement.[33] Numerous occasions to provide feedback should be integrated into your training sessions. This feedback can be provided not only by the instructor but by other trainees as well.

When trainees return to their academic course work, they will likely encounter the same pressures that motivated haphazard research and writing techniques as before (e.g., time pressures, competition, and stress). These pressures may result in a relapse to their pretraining behaviors. Modeled on a tool to support addicts who experience relapse, Marx[34] created a relapse prevention system for trainees. This system informs

Text Box 7.1   Framework on Critically Evaluating Information Resources

The ABCs of Evaluating Information Resources

When evaluating information, consider the following four criteria:

- Authority
- Bias
- Content
- Currency

Authority
Does this person/group know what they are talking about?

Why should you care?

It can be pretty easy to get published. It is important to determine whether the author of a work is credible and knowledgeable about the field. Provide your reader with accurate information.

Tips for evaluating authority:

- What are the author's credentials?
- For which type of audience do the authors write?
- Do they have a record of conducting research in this area?

Bias
Is the research objective? Is it all opinion or are there facts?

Why should you care?

If research is biased, you may be missing an entire side of an issue and not obtaining all of the information needed to present an accurate and clear picture. Sources should be based on research rather than opinion.

How can you tell whether a resource is objective?

- Read through the work and consider its content. Does it appear to represent only one side of an issue?
- Does it disregard pertinent information?

Content
Is the information useful to your research topic?

Why should you care?

Your time is valuable. You don't want to waste time on a resource that either is repeating information that you already have or provides information on a superficial level.

How can you tell if a resource has useful content?

- Is the research relevant to your topic?
- Does it provide new information?
- How does it relate to existing literature on the topic?
- Are the author's arguments convincing?

Currency
Is the information current?

Why should you care?

Older information may have been superseded by new research. Provide your reader with current and accurate information. Note: There may be times when you need to include older research (e.g., an individual founded a theory 50 years ago on which all other research has been based).

How can you tell if a work is current?

- Check the publication date.
- If using a source from the Web, locate a date on the website.
  - o The date can indicate when the information either was initially published or last updated. Ideally, you want to verify when the site was last updated. You can also do this by looking at the dates when an announcement or document was posted.
  - o Check the links. Are the links current and pointing to existing pages? If links lead you to an error message, there is a good chance that the owner is not updating the site frequently.

trainees that relapse will likely occur, identifies situations that may trigger a relapse, and prompts trainees to develop relapse prevention strategies. We adapted Marx's[35] system to the context of plagiarism instruction (see table 7.2)

In combination with goal setting, relapse prevention strategies have been found to improve transfer of training.[36] When a group of trainees meet and discuss goals to implement training in their performance contexts, this has a strong and positive impact on behavior change for a number of reasons. By discussing goals with one another, trainees make a public commitment to change their behavior. Further, through the process of discussing their goals, trainees consider and develop strategies to achieve these goals, increasing the likelihood of implementation.

There are also a number of organizational-level mechanisms that can increase training transfer. The support of the immediate supervisor or, in the case of plagiarism instruction, the instructor, is critical in providing the appropriate support and feedback to trainees who exhibit the correct research and writing behavior.[37] If the culture of the institution emphasizes this behavior, it may stimulate social pressure, which can further reinforce behavior change among trainees. Finally, organizational

Table 7.2.   Plagiarism Relapse Prevention Strategies

Strategy	Explanation
1. Raise student awareness of the relapse process	Conduct discussions encouraging students to describe circumstances that give rise to plagiarism in detail. Heighten participants' awareness of these situations so that they can decrease anxiety and increase the ability to respond to these situations in the future.
2. Recognize situations that give rise to plagiarism	This discussion will prime students to recognize common situations where they may be tempted to plagiarize. Many students will have commonalities when it comes to these situations: time pressure, task overload, academic competition, and so on.
3. Cultivate management skills	While many students may be able to anticipate circumstances leading to relapse, they may struggle to identify proactive behavioral responses in these circumstances. Management skills that can help students cope in these high-risk situations include developing a detailed completion plan for assignments with actions and specific deadlines, consulting with instructors as well as library and writing center personnel, incorporating plagiarism prevention techniques into note-taking practices, and so on.
4. Develop self-efficacy	Encourage students to identify successful application of PEAT program and plagiarism prevention training skills in low-risk situations. Identify examples of unsuccessful implementation in high-risk situations. Emphasize student ability and success in low-risk situations and student potential to transfer this ability with practice to high-risk situations.
5. Consider and prioritize the long-term benefits over the short-term costs	In the short term, students who are integrating new research techniques to avoid plagiarism may find this burdensome and question whether it outweighs the short-term gains of plagiarizing an assignment. Typically, students overfocus on short-term gains and underfocus on the penalties that can be associated with these gains. Discuss both the benefits and the consequences of plagiarism in the short term and the benefits and consequences of new research techniques in the long term. Discuss how the benefit–cost ratio (increased time for seemingly similar or lower rewards) of implementing new research techniques on assignments will improve with practice and over time.

(continued)

Table 7.2. *(continued)*

Strategy	Explanation
6. Abstinence violation effect	The abstinence violation effect occurs when students relapse, feel guilty, and use the relapse to abandon the pursuit of plagiarism avoidance and/or reformed research behaviors. This typically leads to students who plagiarize and feel terrible about it. Discuss this effect with students. Prepare them for the psychological phenomenon that accompanies relapse. Raise their attention to gaining skills from the relapse in order to avoid recurrences in the future.
7. Slippery slopes	Discuss with students minor and seemingly inconsequential choices that may lead to plagiarism behavior. For example, a student might copy and paste from a source with the intent to paraphrase this content before submission. However, when time pressure kicks in, the student fails to paraphrase. Another example might include a student asking to look at a friend's paper for ideas that he or she copies into his or her own paper with the intent of modifying and adapting it later. Again, when time pressure kicks in, the student fails to adapt this content to his or her own work.
8. Stress management skills	Writing research assignments can cause a great deal of stress for students. Discuss emotional and physical stress management activities that can help students endure the effects of this stress.
9. Planned relapse	Ask students to practice failure. One method to achieve this is having students role-play a scenario where they feel pressure to submit a plagiarized paper and asking students to identify their rationalization for plagiarism and their emotions that accompany this "failure." Another method might be to ask students to implement slippery-slope choices that result in plagiarism behavior and discuss the outcome and feeling associated with the outcome.

rewards and consequences play a significant role in reinforcing behavior change among trainees. If an instructor does not enforce the university's academic misconduct procedures for incidents of plagiarism, this has a detrimental impact on training transfer. Further, if trainees perceive that students who employ faulty research methods and commit plagiarism are rewarded with high marks, this greatly discourages any training transfer.[38]

ASSESSMENT OF ORGANIZATIONAL-LEVEL OUTCOMES

The fourth level of Kirkpatrick's[39] training evaluation is assessing what final results have occurred stemming from participation in the training program. Typically, these outcomes concern organizational-level results, such as quality, productivity, reduction in errors, and cost savings or return on investment. More often than not, these questions are not answered in the evaluation of a training program because most trainers do not know how to measure training results and compare them against overall program costs. When we first design plagiarism instruction training, most of it is with specific behaviors in mind that we'd like to address with a larger purpose—to address specific institutional outcomes, such as increasing writing quality among students, decreasing the frequency of academic conduct violations pertaining to plagiarism, reducing the amount of instructor and staff time invested in plagiarism incidents, and decreasing the amount of writing center staff time invested in coaching students about plagiarism. These outcomes will result in clear financial savings and benefits for your institution. In the first three levels of training evaluation (described in chapter 6 and the first part of this chapter), you have learned whether you were successful in shaping the attitudes, knowledge, and skills of your trainees with plagiarism instruction. By assessing organizational-level outcomes, you determine if your training program achieved outcomes that benefit the institution overall.[40]

HOW TO MEASURE ORGANIZATIONAL-LEVEL OUTCOMES

Kirkpatrick[41] suggests six guidelines for evaluating organizational-level outcomes that are similar to his guidelines for evaluating behavior: use a control group, allow time for change to occur, evaluate before and after training, repeat evaluations to gauge change into the future, weigh the costs versus the benefits of the evaluation, and in the absence of concrete proof, recognize the value of the evidence presented. We will limit our discussion here to how these guidelines apply to level 4 evaluation specifically.

Again, if it is possible, you should utilize a control group. Rather than looking at behavioral differences between members of the control group and treatment groups here, you will examine organizational-level outcomes, such as quality of writing or research or aggregate rates of plagiarism across the groups. To evaluate organizational-level results of plagiarism instruction, you might consider looking at plagiarism rates for two research assignments in junior-level classes in different colleges where one college received plagiarism instruction and the other did not. It is strategic to choose your treatment and control groups from colleges that exhibit similar rates of plagiarism. Students enrolled in programs such as business, engineering, and law may be ideal for these purposes. Research has shown that students in professional degree programs (e.g., business, engineering, and law) lag behind those in humanities programs in ethical performance and perceptions.[42] This may result in higher levels of plagiarism in these programs.

As was the case in evaluating behavioral change, time must pass before we can evaluate organizational results.[43] How many trainees must exhibit behavioral change before plagiarism rates meaningfully decrease in the treatment group (or college)? This likely requires trainees to complete multiple writing assignments before you can evaluate these results. The number of writing assignments varies by subject area,[44] and this impacts the timing of your data collection. For example, if you are examining students enrolled in social studies or English courses, it is likely that you can evaluate results after one to two months. However, in math or the sciences, you may have to wait five to seven months before you can collect these data.

It is easier to measure organizational outcomes before and after training than is the case with the level 3 evaluation of behavior.[45] Universities and colleges track academic conduct code violations by department, and you can typically access student performance data from writing instructors. Additionally, writing centers that provide coaching to students often track information about student areas of study, enrolled courses, and specific assignments for which they seek assistance. These data can help you compare the situation before and after your plagiarism instruction program.

As with behavioral change, you must determine how frequently to evaluate organizational outcomes. Perhaps after your first assessment, you discover that plagiarism rates across your trainees actually *increased* following training. This may have more to do with a change in the curriculum than it does with the success or failure of plagiarism instruction. Once trainees have adjusted to that change and continue to advance in their degree programs, it may be worth assessing plagiarism rates again.

Typically, it costs less to evaluate organizational results than behaviors because the numbers that you need are usually available from the institution.[46] The challenge is determining which numbers are available and how your training can directly or indirectly impact these numbers. If this is an ongoing training program that will be repeated multiple times over several semesters, organizational results will likely accrue over a period of time. This may warrant spending more on this level of evaluation, particularly if the organizational results are important to the institution.[47]

When examining organizational-level outcomes, it's almost impossible to claim that your training program is solely responsible for the improvements or declines that you observe. Usually, an alternative explanation can be used to account for these trends. For example, should you observe a decrease in plagiarism rates at your institution for a period of three semesters following your plagiarism instruction, this information provides evidence that your training has had a positive organizational impact. However, these trends could also be explained by an increase in ACT Verbal scores among incoming freshman and transfer students during this same period. In other words, more often than not, organizational-level outcomes provide *evidence* of training success, but we usually cannot equate this evidence with *proof* of training success.[48] This is a significant limitation of level 4 training evaluations. Nonetheless, most decision makers and managers are satisfied by evidence of training success at the organizational level, as they usually are presented only with trainee reactions.[49]

SAMPLE MEASURES OF ORGANIZATIONAL-LEVEL OUTCOMES OF TRAINING

In the previous paragraphs, we've referred to several possible measures of organizational-level outcomes of your plagiarism instruction program. Here we have created a taxonomy of possible measures where we look at a variety of information sources, ranging from class instructors to university administrators. For each source, we suggest direct and indirect measures[50] that may be useful in measuring outcomes of interest. Each of these sources is depicted in the tables 7.3, 7.4, 7.5, and 7.6.

Table 7.3. Organizational Outcomes in the Classroom

Source	Class Instructor (a writing-intensive class or a class with one or more high-stakes research assignments)
Direct measures	1. Distribution of grades on high-stakes writing assignments 2. Change in grade distribution between first and last high-stakes writing assignments 3. Originality scores on high-stakes writing assignments 4. Change in originality scores between first and last high-stakes writing assignments
Indirect measures	1. Student survey questions about research strategy: • Did you use resources from the library to write your paper? • Did you acknowledge all resources that you used with in-text citations in your paper? 2. Student survey questions about note-taking strategy: • Did you take notes from your resources when researching for this paper? • Did you paraphrase all notes that you took when researching for this paper? • Did you include source information on your notes when researching for this paper? 3. Student survey questions about citation techniques: • Did you use APA style to document your resources in the reference section of this paper? • Did you use APA style for your in-text citations in this paper? • Did you include quotation marks and an APA style citation for all direct quotes in your paper? 4. Faculty survey questions about research quality: • Did the research quality of papers improve this semester compared with past semesters? • Did the research quality of papers improve from the beginning to the end of the semester? 5. Faculty survey questions about plagiarism rates: • Did plagiarism rates decrease this semester compared with past semesters? • Did plagiarism rates decrease from the beginning to the end of the semester?

Table 7.4. Organizational Outcomes in the Department

Source	Depending on the size of the school, the source here is a department head, dean or associate dean, or assurance of learning committee members responsible for assessing student performance on research or writing.
Direct measures	1. Distribution of grades in writing-intensive courses 2. Change in distribution of grades in writing-intensive courses from semester to semester 3. Number of plagiarism incidents reported by instructors by semester 4. Change in number of plagiarism incidents reported by instructors from semester to semester

Indirect measures	1. Administrator survey questions about research quality:
	  • Did grades in writing-intensive courses improve this semester compared with past semesters?
	2. Administrator survey questions about plagiarism rates:
	  • Did plagiarism rates decrease this semester compared with past semesters?
	  • Did the severity of plagiarism decrease this semester compared with past semesters?

Table 7.5. Organizational Outcomes in the Writing Center

Source	Many universities have one or more writing centers to offer coaching and support to students working on writing and research assignments. The director of the writing center will likely be the best source for direct measures where individual coaches will be able to provide responses for indirect measures.
Direct measures	1. Percentage of time spent on research quality (e.g., quality of information or lack of resources) during student sessions 2. Percentage of time spent on resource documentation (e.g., missing acknowledgments of resources in paper or missing listings in reference section) during student sessions 3. Percentage of time spent on format of resource documentation (e.g., MLA or APA) during student sessions 4. Percentage of time spent on plagiarism issues (e.g., Overall Similarity Index scores or abrupt changes in writing tone or language suggesting existence of plagiarism) during student sessions

Indirect measures	1. Writing coach survey questions about research quality:
	  • Did research quality of papers improve this semester compared with past semesters?
	  • Did research quality of papers improve from the beginning to the end of the semester?
	2. Writing coach survey questions about plagiarism rates:
	  • Did plagiarism rates decrease this semester compared with past semesters?
	  • Did plagiarism rates decrease from the beginning to the end of the semester?

Table 7.6. Organizational Outcomes in the University

Source	There are a number of administrative units that can provide information about university outcomes. The Office of Student Affairs will likely have data about violations of academic conduct code pertaining to plagiarism. The provost's office or planning and analysis unit should have data about student performance in writing courses. If a writing course is a university requirement for all students, a university curriculum committee may have data about performance in these classes.
Direct measures	1. Distribution of grades in writing-intensive courses 2. Change in distribution of grades in writing-intensive courses from semester to semester 3. Number of plagiarism incidents reported by department by semester 4. Change in number of plagiarism incidents reported by department from semester to semester 5. Average Overall Similarity Index score across the university by semester 6. Change in average Overall Similarity Index score across the university from semester to semester 7. Return on investment: • Do the benefits from items 1 to 6 justify the expenses of plagiarism instruction?

Indirect measures	1. Administrator survey questions about research quality:
	  • Did grades in writing-intensive courses improve this semester compared with past semesters?
	2. Administrator survey questions about plagiarism rates:
	  • Did plagiarism rates decrease this semester compared with past semesters?
	  • Did the severity of plagiarism decrease this semester compared with past semesters?
	3. Administrator survey questions about staff time:
	  • Has the amount of staff time dedicated to plagiarism incidents decreased this semester compared with past semesters?

For each of these sources, you want to collect data from treatment and control groups so that you can use comparisons between the groups as evidence that your plagiarism instruction is effective.

The suggested direct and indirect measures depicted in the tables are meant as a starting point and do not represent a complete list. When selecting organizational outcome measures, you must consider the size and scale of your training program relative to the size and priorities of your organization. One direct measure that has received increasing attention in the past couple of decades in training literature and more recently in library sciences is *return on investment* (ROI). The complexity in calculating ROI, in combination with its increased regard among researchers and practitioners, warrants further discussion.

ROI

Sometimes viewed as a *fifth* level of training evaluation, ROI is aimed at examining the value of a training program from financial and nonfinancial perspectives using both qualitative and quantitative data to determine whether the benefits derived from the training program outweigh its costs.[51] The calculation of ROI, like the other levels of training evaluation, starts in the planning phase of training. Table 7.7, adapted from Phillips,[52] illustrates the type of data that should be collected and considered in the calculation of ROI. Note that if you conduct levels 1 through 4 of Kirkpatrick's training evaluation, you will have already collected the bulk of data necessary to calculate your program's ROI.

After additionally factoring in the direct and indirect costs of planning, delivering, and evaluating the plagiarism instruction program (level 0 in table 7.7), the next step is to *isolate the effects of your program*.[53] This can be achieved through several methods, such as the use of a control group and pre- and posttraining performance comparisons, the use of participant estimates where trainees review their pre- and posttraining performance scores and estimate what percentage of improvement is related to plagiarism instruction, and the use of instructor estimates where instructors consider the performance of trainees and estimate what percentage of improvement is related to plagiarism instruction.[54] Each of these methods helps pinpoint the impact that plagiarism instruction has had on key outcome variables.

The next step to calculate ROI is to convert these data to monetary values.[55] This is an onerous but necessary step in order to determine whether the benefits of your PEAT program outweigh its costs. See Phillips's detailed instructions on calculating ROI in the *ASTD Handbook for Workplace Learning Professionals*.[56]

After converting your data to monetary values, you can calculate your benefit–cost ratio and ROI as a percentage using the formulas provided in the ROI section of Table 7.7. While these numbers indicate the monetary benefits of your plagiarism instruction, you should also consider the nonmonetary, intangible benefits of your program that may provide great value to your organization.[57] These benefits might include increased student and instructor satisfaction with and commitment to the university, increased ethical sensitivity and behaviors as students and alumni, and a reputation for instilling ethical values and behavior in the university's students and employees. It is difficult to convert these benefits into monetary values, but these benefits may be perceived by campus leadership as important and valuable when assessing the overall impact of your plagiarism instruction program.

Table 7.8 illustrates a sample analysis plan for ROI for a PEAT program offered to 30 business students.

Table 7.7. Sample Data Collection for Return on Investment (ROI) Analysis

Data Types	Examples
Input (level 0)	Input includes all costs to develop and implement the plagiarism instruction program. For example: • How many staff are involved? • How many staff hours are dedicated to planning, implementing, and evaluating training? • What is the cost of materials, space, and technology used in developing, delivering, and evaluating training?
Reactions (level 1)	How do trainees react to the plagiarism instruction program? For example: • Is the plagiarism instruction relevant? • Is the plagiarism instruction useful? • Is the plagiarism instruction important? • Is the plagiarism instruction engaging?
Learning (level 2)	Did trainees gain knowledge and skills from the plagiarism instruction program? For example: • Do trainees understand why plagiarism is an ethical issue? • Do trainees know how to avoid committing plagiarism? • Do trainees understand the consequences of committing plagiarism?
Behavior (level 3)	Do trainees implement learning in their academic behavior following plagiarism instruction? For example: • Do trainees paraphrase their notes when researching for written assignments? • Do trainees use appropriate citation format to acknowledge their resources? • Do trainees employ note-taking strategies consistently? • Do trainees employee citation format techniques consistently? • Do trainees receive higher paper marks when employing these strategies?
Results (level 4)	What university outcomes result from plagiarism instruction? For example: • Have average grades in writing-intensive courses increased in departments where plagiarism instruction is offered? • Have plagiarism rates decreased in departments where plagiarism instruction is offered?
ROI (level 5)	Does the monetary value of plagiarism instruction outweigh the cost of preparing, delivering, and evaluating this program? This can be measured by: • Benefit–cost ratio = (value of program benefits)/(value of program costs) • ROI as a % = [(net value of program benefits)/(value of program costs)] × 100

Table adapted from Jack J. Phillips, "Level Four and Beyond: An ROI Model," in *Evaluating Corporate Training: Models and Issues*, ed. Stephen M. Brown and Constance J. Seidner (Norwell, MA: Kluwer Academic, 1998), 113–40, and Jack J. Phillips, "Return-on-Investment," in *ASTD Handbook for Workplace Learning Professionals*, ed. Elaine Biech (Danvers, MA: ASTD Press, 2008), 555–76.

Table 7.8. Sample Analysis Plan for Return on Investment for a PEAT Program

Performance measure	Number of plagiarism incidents across 30 business students in the semester immediately following the PEAT program
Control measures	Compare plagiarism numbers of PEAT participants with plagiarism numbers of PEAT nonparticipants
Conversion of measures into dollars	Cost per incident of plagiarism: conversion using amount of time spent per incident of plagiarism and hourly wage for each individual involved in the plagiarism investigation
Expense categories	Trainer salary Program materials Evaluation cost Facilities (if off campus) Planning and coordination
Nonfinancial benefits	Instructor perceptions of student honesty University reputation Perceptions of student academic performance Interdisciplinary collaboration among instructors and trainers
Feedback loop	University leadership Curriculum committee Academic unit leadership Primary course instructors Intervention developers Participants Instruction content suppliers Community and society
Other considerations	Is some PEAT program content provided in other courses? Equal and independent treatment and control groups (Are there significant pretraining difference between your treatment and control groups? Are they talking to each other about the training?) Timing of PEAT program workshops

NOTES

1. Donald L. Kirkpatrick, *Evaluating Training Programs: The Four Levels* (San Francisco: Berrett-Koehler, 1994), 19.

2. Ibid., 48.

3. Ibid.

4. Ibid., 49.

5. Ibid., 40.

6. Ibid., 41.

7. Ibid., 53.

8. Ibid., 55.

9. Kim Parker, Amanda Lenhart, and Kathleen Moore, "The Digital Revolution and Higher Education: College Presidents, Public Differ on Value of Online Learning," 2011, http://www.pewinternet.org/files/old-media//Files/Reports/2011/PIP-Online-Learning.pdf.

10. Icek Ajzen, "The Theory of Planned Behavior," *Organizational Behavior and Human Decision Processes* 50, no. 2 (1991): 179–211, http://www.sciencedirect.com/science/article/pii/074959789190020T.

11. Thomas H. Stone, I. M. Jawahr, and Jennifer L. Kisamore, "Predicting Academic Misconduct Intentions and Behavior Using the Theory of Planned Behavior and Personality," *Basic and Applied Social Psychology* 32, no. 1 (2010): 45, http://www.tandfonline.com/doi/pdf/10.1080/01973530903539895.

12. Turnitin.com, "Turnitin Effectiveness in U.S. Colleges and Universities." *Turnitin Research Study* [online] (2014), 6.

13. Tracy Bretag and Saadia Mahmud, "A Model for Determining Student Plagiarism: Electronic Detection and Academic Judgement," *Journal of University Teaching & Learning Practice* 6, no. 1 (2009), 54, http://ro.uow.edu.au/jutlp/vol6/iss1/6.

14. Ibid.

15. Donald L. Kirkpatrick and James D. Kirkpatrick, *Transferring Learning to Behavior: Using the Four Levels to Improve Performance* (San Francisco: Berrett-Koehler, 2005), 18.

16. P. Nick Blanchard and James W. Thacker, *Effective Training: Systems, Strategies, and Practices* (Upper Saddle River, NJ: Prentice Hall, 1999), 203.

17. Kirkpatrick and Kirkpatrick, *Transferring Learning to Behavior*, 12.

18. Ibid., 14–15.

19. Robert A. Harris, *The Plagiarism Handbook: Strategies for Preventing, Detecting, and Dealing with Plagiarism* (Los Angeles: Pyrczak Publishing, 2001), 2–12.

20. Kirkpatrick and Kirkpatrick, *Transferring Learning to Behavior*, 12–15.

21. Blanchard and Thacker, *Effective Training*, 207.

22. Ibid., 207–12.

23. Ibid., 204; James C. Naylor and George E. Briggs, "Effects of Rehearsal of Temporal and Spatial Aspects on the Long-Term Retention of a Procedural Skill," *Journal of Applied Psychology* 47, no. 2 (1963), 120–26, http://dx.doi.org/10.1037/h0040215.

24. Blanchard and Thacker, *Effective Training*, 204; Timothy T. Baldwin and J. Kevin Ford, "Transfer of Training: A Review and Directions for Future Research," *Personnel Psychology* 41, no. 1 (1998): 63–105, doi:10.1111/j.1744-6570.1988.tb00632.x.

25. Blanchard and Thacker, *Effective Training*, 204–5.

26. Ibid., 205.

27. William McGhee and Paul W. Thayer, *Training in Business and Industry* (New York: Wiley, 1961), 176–78.

28. Joseph D. Hagman and Andrew M. Rose, "Retention of Military Tasks: A Review," *Human Factors* 25, no. 2 (1983): 199–214, http://hfs.sagepub.com/content/25/2/199.abstract.

29. Blanchard and Thacker, *Effective Training*, 205.

30. Ibid., 206.

31. Ibid.

32. Kirkpatrick and Kirkpatrick, *Transferring Learning to Behavior*, 64.

33. Blanchard and Thacker, *Effective Training*, 207; Edwin A. Locke and Gary P. Latham, *A Theory of Goal Setting and Task Performance* (Upper Saddle River, NJ: Prentice Hall, 1990), 17–18.

34. Robert D. Marx, "Relapse Prevention for Managerial Training: A Model for Maintenance of Behavior Change," *Academy of Management Review* 7, no. 3(1982): 440, http://www.jstor.org/stable/257336.

35. Ibid.

36. Blanchard and Thacker, *Effective Training*, 207; Michael Feldman, "Successful Post Training Skill Application," *Training and Development Journal*, September 1981, 72–75; Kenneth N. Wexley and Timothy T. Baldwin, "Posttraining Strategies for Facilitating Positive Transfer: An Empirical Exploration," *Academy of Management Journal* 29, no. 3 (1986): 503–20, http://www.jstor.org/stable/256221.

37. Blanchard and Thacker, *Effective Training*, 209; Kirkpatrick and Kirkpatrick, *Transferring Learning to Behavior*, 67.

38. Blanchard and Thacker, *Effective Training*, 210; Kirkpatrick and Kirkpatrick, *Transferring Learning to Behavior*, 77.

39. Kirkpatrick, *Evaluating Training Programs*, 19.

40. Ibid., 25.

41. Ibid., 61.

42. Bob S. Brown, "A Comparison of the Academic Ethics of Graduate Business, Education, and Engineering Students," *College Student Journal* 30, no. 3 (1996): 294–301; Donald D. Carpenter, Trevor S. Harding, Cynthia J. Finelli, Susan M. Montgomery, and Honor J. Passow, "Engineering Students' Perceptions of and Attitudes towards Cheating," *Journal of Engineering Education* 95, no. 3 (2006): 181–94, http://onlinelibrary.wiley.com/doi/10.1002/j.2168-9830.2006.tb00891.x/abstract; Trevor S. Harding, Matthew J. Mayhew, Cynthia J. Finelli, and Donald D. Carpenter, "The Theory of Planned Behavior as a Model of Academic Dishonesty in Humanities and Engineering Undergraduates," *Ethics and Behavior* 17, no. 3 (2007): 255–79, http://www.tandfonline.com/doi/full/10.1080/10508420701519239; Donald L. McCabe and Linda Klebe Trevino, "Individual and Contextual Influences on Academic Dishonesty: A Multicampus Investigation," *Research in Higher Education* 38, no. 3 (1997): 379–96, http://www.jstor.org/stable/40196302.

43. Kirkpatrick, *Evaluating Training Programs*, 62.

44. ACT Research and Policy, "ACT National Curriculum Survey®: High School and College Educators' Estimates of the Number of Long Writing Assignments in Their Courses," *Information Brief 2014-3* (2014): 1368

45. Kirkpatrick, *Evaluating Training Programs*, 62.

46. Ibid., 63.

47. Ibid.

48. Ibid., 61.

49. Ibid., 65.

50. Barbara E. Walvoord, "Assessment Clear and Simple: Practical Steps for Institutions, Departments, and General Education," *Assessment Institute in Indianapolis* (October 2015), 12.

51. Jack J. Phillips, "Level Four and Beyond: An ROI Model," in *Evaluating Corporate Training: Models and Issues*, ed. Stephen M. Brown and Constance J. Seidner (Norwell, MA: Kluwer Academic, 1998), 113–40; Jack J. Phillips, "Return-on-Investment," in *ASTD Handbook for Workplace Learning Professionals*, ed. Elaine Biech (Danvers, MA: ASTD Press, 2008): 555–76.

52. Phillips, "Return-on-Investment," 558.

53. Ibid., 566.

54. Ibid., 566–67.

55. Ibid., 567–69.

56. Ibid., 569.

57. Ibid., 570.

8

Sharing the News

Communicating Your Training Results

Once you have finally completed the evaluation of your training program, you must determine what to do with this information. Your evaluation data may be critical in driving the improvement of your plagiarism instruction program. In addition to using your results to inform modifications and improvements in the design and delivery of training, you should consider with whom you will share your evaluation data. The communication of your evaluation results is just as important as achieving these results.[1]

COMMUNICATING EVALUATION RESULTS

In the context of communicating the results of your plagiarism prevention instruction program, your audience is comprised of any prospective user of evaluation results and other stakeholders who may be potentially influenced by these results.[2] Drawing on Cummings's research on corporate stakeholders,[3] we identified eight potential stakeholder groups who have a vested interest in the results of plagiarism prevention instruction at higher-education institutions:

1. University leadership: Those who are responsible for the overall performance of the institution.
2. Curriculum committee (within each academic unit): Those who make decisions at the departmental level to set and assess progress toward curriculum/instruction goals.
3. Academic unit leadership: Those at the departmental level who make budget allocations for stand-alone writing classes and plagiarism workshops.

4. Primary course instructors: Those who collaborate with Plagiarism and Ethics Awareness Training (PEAT) program instructors and who allocate class time for PEAT sessions.

5. Intervention developers: Those responsible for designing the PEAT program. More often than not, intervention developers will also deliver the instruction.

6. Participants: Typically, students who invest time and effort to participate in a PEAT program.

7. Instruction content suppliers: Individuals or other organizations that offer products or services that are necessary components in the design and delivery of a PEAT session.

8. Communities and society: These larger entities benefit from successful PEAT programs. As we cited in chapter 4, research has found that students who commit unethical academic acts at university are more likely to commit unethical acts in the workplace. According to a 2015 report from the National Business Ethics Surveys, 51 percent of employees in large companies (with 90,000 or more employees) report that they observe misconduct in the workplace.[4] Although this number represents improvement from past years, the fact that this number represents a majority of employees (in large companies) indicates that communities and society stand to gain much from improvement in this area.

Although we have identified several potential stakeholder groups, Phillips[5] asserts that senior management (university and department leadership), supervisors of trainees (course instructors and writing center coaches), trainees (student participants), and training staff (those who develop and deliver the training) should always receive your return-on-investment (ROI) data. University and department leadership should receive your ROI data, as they have an interest in these outcomes as well as potential influence to allocate more or fewer resources to support your prevention program. Instructors and writing center coaches should receive this information, as their support is critical to reinforcing the behavioral outcomes of your plagiarism prevention instruction. Students need to understand what was accomplished by this training, and ROI data may further reinforce their commitment to behavioral change and support of the training program. Finally, training staff can use ROI data to better understand the ROI process and consider design and implementation changes that may enhance ROI.[6]

In addition to carefully selecting your audience, several principles shape how you communicate your results:[7]

1. Communications should be timely: Generally, results should be communicated as soon as they are known. However, for practical reasons, you might delay communication until it is convenient for your audience. You might also consider timing your communication so that your audience is ready or more receptive to your results. For example, when preparing to communicate results to your department heads and deans, you must consider when they meet and

what pressing issues are on their agendas. If at their next meeting they will be making contentious budgetary decisions, they may not be receptive or attentive to the training results that you present. In this situation, it would be wise to postpone your presentation until after they resolve the sensitive budgeting dispute and can devote more attention to the information that you present.

2. Communications should be tailored to specific audiences: For example, writing instructors and writing center coaches will likely be more concerned with attitudinal and behavioral changes among trainees, whereas department heads, deans, and other administrators will be more attentive to organizational-level outcomes and ROI. What you communicate to each of these audiences should be tailored to these differing interests.

3. Appropriate communication channels and/or media should be used for specific audiences: For audiences with limited time, such as university leadership, a memo may be more effective and efficient than a face-to-face presentation. For training participants who may be hard to reassemble after the conclusion of the semester, a digital presentation, such as a video, PowerPoint, or interactive Web-based report, will likely be more practical and effective than a written report or in-person meeting. For instructors, coaches, and department leadership, a face-to-face meeting may result in more effective communication than a paper or digital report. By choosing the appropriate channel to communicate your results, you increase the overall effectiveness of this process.

4. Communications should be impartial and restrained: Including opinions that might overstate the significance or importance of your training outcomes can alienate your audience members. Let your results speak for themselves. This will increase the perceived credibility of your plagiarism prevention program, your program results, and you.

5. Communications should be regular and reliable: The schedule and substance of your communication should not deviate from any established precedents. If you typically report training results at the winter faculty retreat, you should keep with this practice. By introducing a sudden change in the timing of these results, you may raise apprehension in your target audience. It's important to maintain consistent communication even when you have bad results to report. This will increase trust among your target audience members: "Even though plagiarism prevention instruction was less effective this year, the trainers still shared these results with us. I can count on them to report both good and bad outcomes."

6. Communications should anticipate the preferences and perceptions of their specific audience: Consider the relationship you have with your target audience. If you have a positive relationship and a strong sense that they are supportive of the PEAT program, you may have an easier job of preparing and delivering your results. If you have a combative history with a target audience, they may be resistant to the facts and information that you communicate to them. The latter audience represents a more challenging situation for which to

prepare and deliver communications. One strategy you might consider in this situation is enlisting partners (who have more favorable relations with your target) in the communication of your training results. Another tactic you can take is to tailor the presentation of your results to emphasize areas of key interest to the combative target group.

7. Communications should be carefully planned: In order to maximize the outcomes of your plagiarism prevention instruction, you must plan to ensure that each of your target audiences gets the information they need at the right time in order to follow up with the appropriate response (whether that be recruiting future trainee participants from their classes or dedicating funding for future training sessions). Phillips and colleagues[8] recommend that the following factors warrant attention when planning communication of training results:
   - What is the substance of your communication?
   - When will you communicate it?
   - How will you communicate it?
   - Where will your communication occur?
   - Who will be responsible for communicating it?
   - Who is your target audience(s)?
   - How do you hope your audience(s) will respond to the communication? What outcomes do you desire as a result of this communication?

Broslawsky[9] recommends including the following when reporting your results:

1. Executive summary.
2. General information about the PEAT program and the purpose of the training evaluation.
3. Methodology for the training evaluation. Sharing this with your audience builds credibility for the evaluation process. Discuss the levels of evaluation, how you collected data, any control group comparisons and pre/posttraining assessment, and how you converted data into dollar amounts to calculate ROI.
4. General results, such as who responded to your evaluations and whether you achieved the general objectives of the PEAT program.
5. Level 1 evaluation results: What were the reactions of trainees? How did you collect your data? What do the data tell us? Were there any issues or challenges at this level of assessment?
6. Level 2 evaluation results: What did trainees learn? How did you collect your data? What do the data tell us? Were there any issues or challenges at this level of assessment?
7. Level 3 evaluation results: Did trainees change behaviors? How did you collect your data? What do the data tell us? Were there any issues or challenges at this level of assessment?
8. Level 4 evaluation results: What was the organizational impact of the PEAT program? How did you collect your data? What do the data tell us? Were there any issues or challenges at this level of assessment?

9. Level 5 evaluation results: What was the ROI of the PEAT program, and what does this mean in practical terms?
10. Are there any additional intangible outcomes of the PEAT program?
11. Conclusion: What do you conclude from this assessment, and what do you recommend based on this assessment?
12. Appendices, tables, and figures.

FEEDBACK LOOPS

Ultimately, the purpose of conducting an evaluation of your PEAT program is to improve the training process. It is with this goal in mind that we design, implement, and analyze the results from the training evaluation. This goal also drives how we communicate the results of the program evaluation to target audiences.[10] However, how we communicate our evaluation results depends on the nature of these results. If we have successful results to report, this drives a different messaging strategy than if we have moderate to unsuccessful results to report. When we have negative training results to report, we want to engage audiences and involve them in taking a thorough and critical look at the content and implementation of the PEAT program. We need to carefully consider how to mobilize each audience we present to, as they may be critical resources in helping to discover how to achieve desired results from the PEAT program. The following guidelines offer a framework for planning this communication:[11]

1. Focus on the situation: It is easy to fall into the trap of blaming training failures on individuals involved in this training. This does not lead to a productive conversation and will alienate potential collaborators who have valuable insights to help improve the PEAT program. Focus your presentation on the cold, hard fact: *these were the outcomes of the PEAT program, and we did not meet our performance goals.*
2. Demonstrate that you viewed the situation from other perspectives: It is important to share as much data as possible. Use these data to paint as comprehensive a picture as possible with multiple potential causes for the underperformance of the PEAT program.
3. Articulate what these results mean and what will happen if the PEAT program does not improve: How will this impact the training staff? How will it impact you? How will it impact students and other stakeholders? How will it impact future training programs?
4. Demonstrate a willingness to remain open: Solicit input from this group. What went well? What could be improved? What do they need in order to implement improvements?
5. Keep a relaxed and open demeanor: Maintain a calm conversational tone throughout this conversation. This will help you keep the training staff comfortable and engaged in problem solving throughout this discussion.

6. Match your facial expressions to the conversation: Be sure that your nonverbal communication matches the tone and content of your discussion. Are your facial expressions and body gestures as relaxed and open as your tone and your words?

7. Speak calmly and confidently: Finally, you want to speak confidently in addition to calmly. By acting confidently, you can build mutual trust and confidence with the training staff. Not only do you need to engage them with this problem, but you need them to trust you enough to collaborate with you.

Regardless of the positive or negative nature of your training results, you will modify your message for particular audiences based on their roles within the PEAT program and their interests. For example, when we communicate training results to staff who plan, design, and deliver a PEAT program, we do so expecting that trainers will use these results to make the necessary modifications in the design, content, and delivery of instruction to improve training effectiveness. This may also result in a decrease in training costs and an increase in overall training efficiency.

When we communicate training results to PEAT participants, we may seek to remind them of and reinforce what they have learned and what they should be practicing in their course work outside of training: *the success of the PEAT program depends on their follow-through.* Furthermore, communicating results to trainees may serve to recognize and reward them for what they have learned and achieved as a result of their hard work and participation in training.

By communicating results to writing instructors and coaches, we can illustrate what trainees have learned and what role instructors and coaches can play in reinforcing the knowledge and behaviors gained from the PEAT program among trainees. Department and university leadership may view the results from your PEAT program as compelling motivation to renew or increase support for and commitment to this program in the future.

Communicating results to multiple stakeholder groups can demonstrate the value of the program and increase a sense of satisfaction with and success of your PEAT program. This may help market this and other training programs that you provide. It may also support the expansion of the PEAT program to other areas.

The communication of training results and the use of these results to drive future improvement is an important final but often overlooked step in the training evaluation process. In any organization, particularly a large bureaucratic structure that typifies instructions of higher education, it is up to you to demonstrate the value and impact of your programs to all key stakeholder groups. Although plagiarism prevention instruction is likely an important issue to you, it is up to you to demonstrate the importance of this training to PEAT participants and key organizational decision makers. Chapters 6 to 8 are intended to serve as resources to guide you in this task.

NOTES

1. Jack J. Phillips, Patricia Pulliam Phillips, and Toni Krucky Hodges, *Making Training Evaluation Work* (Alexandria, VA: ASTD Press, 2004), 73.

2. Oliver W. Cummings, "What Stakeholders Want to Know," in *Evaluating Corporate Training: Models and Issues*, ed. Stephen M. Brown and Constance J. Seidner (Norwell, MA: Kluwer Academic, 1998), 42.

3. Ibid.

4. Ethics Research Center, "Executive Summary—The State of Ethics in Large Companies," 2015, https://www.ethics.org/newsite/research/eci-research/nbes/nbes-reports/large-companies.

5. Jack J. Phillips, "Level Four and Beyond: An ROI Model," in Brown and Seidner, *Evaluating Corporate Training*, 137.

6. Ibid.

7. Tom Broslawsky, "Reporting Evaluation Results," in *ASTD Handbook of Measuring and Evaluating Training*, ed. Patricia Pulliam Phillips (Danvers, MA: ASTD Press, 2010), 240–42; Phillips, Phillips, and Hodges, *Making Training Evaluation Work*, 74.

8. Phillips et al., *Making Training Evaluation Work*, 75.

9. Broslawsky, "Reporting Evaluation Results," 247.

10. Phillips et al., *Making Training Evaluation Work*, 75–77.

11. Renee Evenson, *Powerful Phrases for Dealing with Difficult People: Over 325 Ready-to-Use Words and Phrases for Working with Challenging Personalities* [e-book] (New York: AMACOM, 2014), chap. 4.

9

Where Do We Go from Here?

A Holistic Model for Plagiarism Prevention

In this book, we extend plagiarism prevention training by incorporating an ethical element targeted toward the intentional plagiarist. The Plagiarism and Ethics Awareness Training (PEAT) program has the potential to advance plagiarism prevention by changing student attitudes toward this behavior. In his review of plagiarism research, Youmans found that 7 to 55 percent of students surveyed freely admit to committing intentional acts of plagiarism.[1] This represents a conservative estimate of intentional plagiarism rates as several students likely chose to provide dishonest responses to this question. When you consider that up to 55 percent of plagiarism violations on college campuses may be intentional, the PEAT program plays an important role in reducing plagiarism rates among students.

Changing student attitudes toward plagiarism is the thrust of the PEAT program. However, we want to emphasize once again that for PEAT to be effective, it must be combined with additional plagiarism prevention training that emphasizes research and writing skills. Particularly in the case of unintentional plagiarists, students need to know how to avoid plagiarism once they come to the conclusion that this behavior is something that is unacceptable and unethical in an academic context.

When we first conceived the idea for an ethics-based plagiarism prevention program, we envisioned that it would be implemented at all levels of a degree program. Due to a variety of obstacles (i.e., resistance by some instructors, tightly scheduled courses, scheduling conflicts, lack of personnel, and so on), we were unable to execute our ambitious curriculum-wide design. However, we believe that a holistic plagiarism prevention program that builds on skills and concepts year after year and that is reinforced throughout a curriculum is a worthy pursuit in the campaign to improve academic and professional ethical behavior. Here, we present and discuss this aspirational model as a future direction for plagiarism prevention instruction that includes attitudes and skills and that is embedded at every level of the curriculum.

Our proposed curriculum-wide model was developed based on the intersection of academic and workplace behavior. Research suggests that there is a positive relationship between academic misconduct and workplace misconduct.[2] Our goal was to develop a curriculum that would address both of these issues. We proposed a four-step approach that would provide instruction to students during their freshman, sophomore, junior, and senior years. See figure 9.1 for a graphical depiction of the curriculum.

We expect this model to be implemented at the college or department level. For this model to work, there must be complete support from the deans and department heads as they would have to help ensure that the trainers receive the class time needed to conduct the training and provide the monetary and human resources needed to implement the program. Recall from chapter 1 our discussion of the four stages of institutionalizing academic integrity. By implementing this model, a college is signaling that (1) it recognizes the academic and professional ethics as a problem (stage 1), (2) it has identified solutions to this problem through the training design (stage 2), and (3) it has committed resources to implementing solutions to this problem (stage 3), which will lead to (4) a full integration of academic integrity into the college (stage 4).[3] Implementing this program supports the goal of institutionalizing academic integrity at your institution where ethical values are integrated completely into the curriculum and faculty, staff, administration, and students are committed to upholding a culture in which academic integrity flourishes.

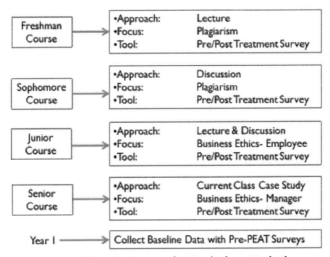

Figure 9.1. Integrating PEAT across the Curriculum: Methods

The first stage of instruction should occur in a required 100-level class. Students will receive instruction on plagiarism prevention strategies. This instruction includes information on what constitutes plagiarism, examples of plagiarism, how to paraphrase and attribute correctly, and note-taking strategies. This first stage of treatment emphasizes the delivery of information to increase awareness of plagiarism among students who as freshmen have a greater likelihood of committing unintentional plagiarism due to a lack of information and/or experience.

Stage 2 should be presented to a core 200-level course in a given discipline using the PEAT method. Students participate in a discussion (or series of discussions) using various scenarios to explore potential acts of plagiarism. This second stage of instruction emphasizes active learning and application of critical thinking by students to recognize and respond to plagiarism scenarios.

Stage 3, which is delivered to a required 300-level course, begins the shift from plagiarism prevention to ethical workplace behavior. During this instruction session, the instructor uses transmissive strategies to discuss the link between dishonesty in academia and dishonesty in a work/professional setting as well as transformative strategies by involving students in case-based discussions.

The final stage is presented to students participating in their senior capstone course and delves deeper into ethical issues that will arise in their future professions. Many of the models used in the PEAT method can be extrapolated to a variety of common professional ethics dilemmas. Here, the instructor will draw primarily on transformative approaches, including case-based discussions and role plays. The Giving Voice to Values framework can also serve as a diagnostic tool for students to guide ethical behavior in these scenarios. As students progress through their academic studies, the importance of academic integrity and its relationship to workplace behavior is continually reinforced through a curriculum-wide model of plagiarism and ethics awareness training.

If this program is implemented across the curriculum in conjunction with careful assessment strategies, plagiarism prevention instructors will have the opportunity to make a compelling case to support or dismiss the effectiveness of training on ethical behavior in both academic and professional contexts. Program evaluation can be implemented at each level, and comparisons can be made between and within course levels (see figures 9.2 and 9.3). Here, it is critical to conduct pre-/postsurveys to evaluate the change in student attitudes toward and behavior within plagiarism and workplace settings. As the program progresses, your college accumulates longitudinal data to measure progress and areas for improvement over time.

Moving from project to program requires a significant investment of time, energy, and resources. Implementers should secure a commitment from college and/or department administration to give the program enough time to develop and adequate time to assess. While there will likely be growing pains during the early stages of the program, it is important to view these challenges as trials, not as failures. They are opportunities to revise and improve the program. Again, support from administration is crucial, and a well-developed plan to assess the program's successes and areas

Integrating PEAT Across a Curriculum: Comparisons *Between* Course Levels

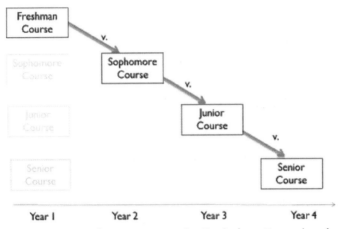

Figure 9.2. Integrating PEAT across the Curriculum: Comparison between Courses

Integrating PEAT Across a Curriculum: Comparisons *Within* Course Level

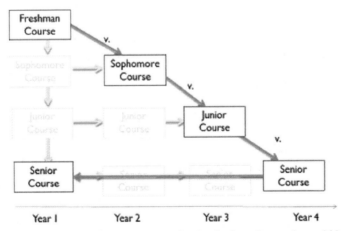

Figure 9.3. Integrating PEAT across the Curriculum: Comparison within Course Levels

needing improvement is necessary to evaluate whether investments in the program are outweighed by returns.

In this book's preface, we included two quotes that presented disheartening student attitudes toward academic integrity. One student indicated that he or she didn't perceive cheating to be unethical behavior, while another student suggested that he or she didn't perceive cheating to be unethical behavior in a university environment. The aim of this book is to provide instructors with a strategy to change these attitudes—to strongly communicate that plagiarism is unacceptable and unethical and will not be overlooked. The more you can integrate this approach across the curriculum, the greater chance you have of creating a culture of academic integrity that trains ethical students to become our future's ethical professionals.

NOTES

1. Robert J. Youmans, "Does the Adoption of Plagiarism-Detection Software in Higher Education Reduce Plagiarism?," *Studies in Higher Education* 36, no. 7 (2011): 749–50.

2. Randi L. Sims, "The Relationship between Academic Dishonesty and Unethical Business Practices," *Journal of Education for Business* 68, no. 4 (1993): 207–11, doi:10.1080/0883 2323.1993.10117614; Raef A. Lawson, "Is Classroom Cheating Related to Business Students' Propensity to Cheat in the 'Real World'?," *Journal of Business Ethics* 49, no. 2 (2004): 189–99, doi:10.1023/B: BUSI.0000015784.34148.cb; Sarath Nonis and Cathy Owens Swift, "An Examination of the Relationship between Academic Dishonesty and Workplace Dishonesty: A Multicampus Investigation," *Journal of Education for Business* 77, no. 2 (2001): 69–77, doi:10.1016/j.paid.2007.03.017.

3. Stephen F. Davis, Patrick F. Drinan, and Tricia Bertram Gallant, *Cheating in School: What We Know and What We Can Do* (Malden, MA: Wiley-Blackwell, 2009), 159.

Appendix

Plagiarism Scenarios

Below are sample scenarios that can be used during an instructional session. Each of these scenarios can be used with any of the modules outlined in chapter 4. Each scenario includes variations providing a different aspect of the issue. Some rewriting may be required to adapt the variations.

SCENARIO 1

Jane is taking a finance class and is assigned a 10- to 15-page paper that requires her to analyze the financial health of a company. The paper accounts for 35 percent of the final grade. Jane is currently interning at a local financial firm and has been quite busy with her internship and other class assignments. Her financial analysis assignment is due in two days. Knowing that she doesn't have time to write a paper, she takes a report from a "report bank" at the firm, reformats it, and turns it in.

Variations of Scenario

    A. Jane tells a student that she is submitting a report written by an analyst at the firm.

    B. A student overhears Jane tell another person that she turned in a report written by an analyst at the firm where she is interning.

    C. Jane tells the student to take a report written by an analyst at the firm where both are interning and submit it as her own for the financial analysis assignment. Jane tells the student she has done it before and has never been caught.

SCENARIO 2

You and your roommate are currently taking different sections of an intermediate sociology class. Both of you have an assignment to write a four-page paper that evaluates a research article on the topic of racial tensions in prison. The assignment is due after spring break. Because you are going to Florida with friends over break, you complete the paper a few days before spring break. Your roommate has been struggling with the class and has been procrastinating on the assignment. About a week after spring break, you notice a paper on your roommate's desk titled "Bigotry behind Bars: Racial Tensions in U.S Prisons: An Evaluation." This is the same paper title you used for your assignment. You look more closely at the paper and realize that she copied and submitted your assignment as her own. You have not yet received a grade for your paper.

Variations of Scenario

    A. You had taken the class the previous semester and had already received a grade.

    B. You offer to show your paper to your roommate to give her an idea of how you approached the assignment.

    C. You are an innocent bystander and completed the course last semester. Your friend tells you that she submitted a paper written by her roommate, who also happens to be a friend of yours.

SCENARIO 3

Susan finds a flash drive in a computer at the library. While trying to identify the owner, she notices that the owner took the same biology course that she is currently taking. The class is assignment intensive with many labs and short papers. Susan has a lab report due this week that has been particularly challenging and is about 50 percent completed. She locates the report that the owner wrote for this particular lab and thinks it is much better. Knowing that it would take her another two hours to complete her own lab report, she decides to submit the report that she found on the flash drive.

Variations of Scenario

    A. Susan knows the owner of the flash drive.

    B. You and Susan are assigned to work together to submit one lab report in which both of you will receive the same grade.

    C. Susan had already completed the lab report but decided to submit the owner's report anyway because it appeared to be better than hers.

SCENARIO 4

Bill buys a course answer booklet for an introductory algebra class. Classmates soon find out that he has the answers to the assignment and begin buying the answers from him.

Variations of Scenario

A. The professor is grading the course on a curve. You have not bought the answers from Bill but are suffering from the consequence because the students who did purchase answers are receiving better grades than you.
B. The department head and professor confront the class about the cheating and threaten to fail everyone in the class unless they learn who is selling the answers.
C. Bill is giving away the answers instead of selling them to students.

SCENARIO 5

Karen is a third-year law student and has only one semester until she graduates. She is taking a course in family law and is writing a 20-page paper on international adoption. Using Lexis and Westlaw, Karen finds articles on her topic. She takes five articles and cuts and pastes the content and footnotes from these articles to assemble a paper.

Variations of Scenario

A. Karen asks you to review her paper. You tell her that it appears to be plagiarized. Karen submits the paper anyway.
B. The dean of the law school is preparing character and fitness reports that will be submitted to the state bar that state that a student has good moral character and can be trusted to uphold the laws of the state. Karen's report is in this pool.
C. Instead of submitting this paper for a course, Karen is submitting the paper to a prestigious competition in which the winner and the school receive national recognition.

Scenarios have been adapted from the following sources:

Harris, Robert A. *The Plagiarism Handbook: Strategies for Preventing, Detecting, and Dealing with Plagiarism.* Los Angeles: Pyrczak Publishing, 2001, 151–52.
Library Instruction Services, University of Texas Libraries and George Schorn. "Avoiding Plagiarism: A Guide for University of Texas Student Mentors." 2008. http://www.lib.utexas.edu/sites/default/files/services/instruction/AvoidingPlagiarism_guide.pdf.

Index

About the Authors

Connie Strittmatter is the head librarian for access services at Boston College. Prior to her position at Boston College, she was the team leader for access services and associate professor at Montana State University Library. She received her MLS from Kent State University in 2000 and her MBA from the W. P. Carey School of Business at Arizona State University in 2004. Connie's research focus has been on pedagogical design for library instruction. She has published in *College & Research Libraries*, the *Journal of Business and Finance Librarianship*, and *Ethics & Behavior*. While at Montana State University, Connie worked with business faculty to incorporate a library instruction module (with an ethics component) into a core business class. She expanded her plagiarism and ethics instruction into engineering and international student orientation.

Virginia K. Bratton is an associate professor of management in the Jake Jabs College of Business and Entrepreneurship at Montana State University. She received her PhD in business administration in 2004 from Florida State University, where she completed her dissertation on the topic of ethical decision making on a student population. Dr. Bratton teaches courses in organizational behavior, human resource management, and leadership. Her research focus is on business ethics, impression management, and performance appraisals, and she has published in the *Journal of Organizational Behavior*, the *Journal of Vocational Behavior*, and the *Leadership and Organization Development Journal*. Dr. Bratton has delivered ethics instruction to a broad array of populations, including undergraduate business and engineering students at Montana State University; doctoral management students at the University of Melbourne, Australia; and human resource management practitioners from Montana and its surrounding states.